T0024942

100 Task Cards
Making Inferences

Reproducible Mini-Passages With Key Questions to Boost Reading Comprehension Skills

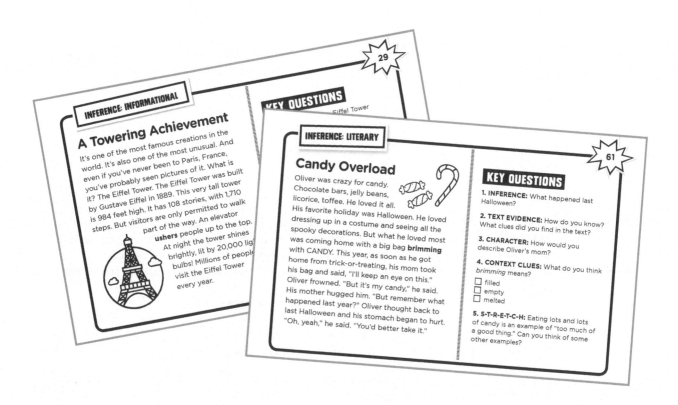

New York • Toronto • London
Auckland • Sydney • New Delhi • Hong Kong

Passages written by Carol Ghiglieri and Justin Martin
Cover design by Tannaz Fassihi
Cover photo © photosindia/Getty Images
Interior illustrations from The Noun Project

ISBN: 978-1-338-60316-3

Scholastic Inc., 557 Broadway, New York, NY 10012
Copyright © 2020 by Scholastic Inc.
Published by Scholastic Inc.
All rights reserved. Printed in the U.S.A.
First printing, January 2020.

7 8 9 10   150   26 25 24 23

CONTENTS

INTRODUCTION

Welcome to *100 Task Cards: Making Inferences*!

Comprehension is more critical than ever. Rigorous state standards mean that students are required to understand a wide variety of informational and literary texts. Challenging students is important, but many are not making the grade because they are failing to master essential reading skills, including the crucial ability to make inferences.

Making inferences requires students to read between the lines and glean the "deep meaning" of a text when that meaning is not explicitly stated. For example, if an article says "sugar can have sour consequences" or a fiction story says "his knees knocked and his heart raced," readers would need sophisticated comprehension skills to unlock the true intent of the author. No doubt about it, a firm grasp of inference is essential to effective reading, writing, test taking, and success in school and beyond. Sound like a tall order? Indeed it is.

But don't despair. *100 Task Cards: Making Inferences* is here to help your students master this tricky skill in just minutes a day! Each card includes an informational or literary mini-passage, along with key questions that give kids plenty of practice making inferences and answering prompts related to:

- **Main Idea and Details**
- **Comparing and Contrasting**
- **Sequence of Events**
- **Summarizing**
- **Character**
- **Setting**
- **Tone**
- **Theme**
- **Predicting**
- **Description**
- **Context Clues**
- **Text Evidence**
- **and more!**

The cards are designed for instant use—just photocopy them and cut them apart, and they're good to go. The cards are also designed for flexible use. They're perfect for seatwork, centers, or meaningful homework. They're great for independent practice or for work with partners, small groups, and even the whole class.

The questions on the cards will help students hone critical comprehension skills they'll rely on for a lifetime. And here's more good news: Because the mini-passages were written by professional authors with a gift for engaging young readers, kids will absolutely *love* them!

So what are you waiting for? Read on for tips that will help your students grow into confident, fluent, "deep" readers—quickly and painlessly. And don't forget to look for the other great *100 Task Cards* books in this series, including *Informational Text, Literary Text, Text Evidence, Context Clues,* and *Figurative Language*. The kids in your class will thank you.

TEACHING TIPS

About the 100 Making Inferences Task Cards

The book contains 100 inference cards, each with a mini-passage; 50 feature informational text and 50 feature literary text. In an effort to give students a rich variety of reading material that correlates with current state standards, the texts vary by topic, form, purpose, and tone. (For a list of the standards these cards address, see page 8.) Each card presents five key questions, including several questions directly related to inference. Each card also includes a context clue. This special feature is intended to boost your students' abilities to glean the meaning of unfamiliar words they encounter in all texts.

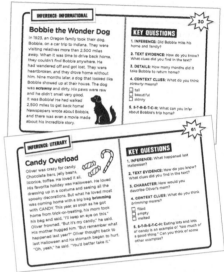

Additionally, the cards variously address the following categories: main idea and details, comparing and contrasting, sequencing, summarizing, character, setting, tone, theme, predicting, citing text evidence, and more. The mini-passages can be used in any order you choose. However, if you are teaching a certain topic or wish to help students hone a particular skill—such as making predictions—you can simply assign one or more cards that include that category.

SAMPLE CARD: Here's a quick tour of a task card.

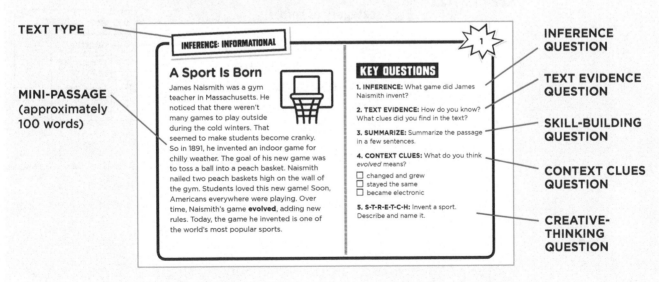

About the 14 Comprehension Helper Cards

To scaffold student learning, we've provided 14 Comprehension Helper cards. (See pages 9–15.) These "bonus" cards, on a range of comprehension topics, are intended to provide grade-perfect background information that will help students respond knowledgeably to the five questions on the 100 task cards. We suggest you photocopy a set for each student to have at the ready.

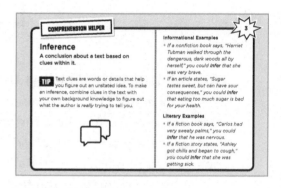

About the Answer Key

We've also included a complete answer key. (See pages 67–80.) In the key, we've provided sample responses to the questions on all 100 cards. Please note that student answers will vary. Because many of the questions are open-ended and no two minds work exactly alike, we encourage you to accept all reasonable answers.

MAKING THE TASK CARDS

The task cards are easy to make. Just photocopy the pages and cut along the dashed lines.

- **Tip #1:** For sturdier cards, photocopy the pages on card stock and/or laminate them.

- **Tip #2:** To make the cards extra appealing, use different colors of paper or card stock for each category of card.

- **Tip #3:** To store the cards, use a plastic lunch bag or a recipe box. Or, hole-punch the corner of each card and place them on a key ring.

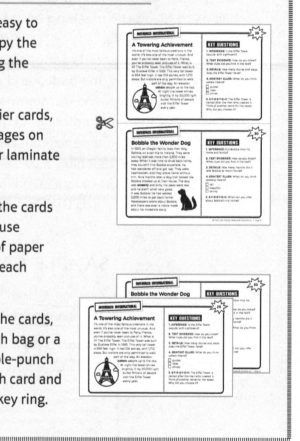

First-Time Teaching Routine

Any text will become accessible to students who bring strong reading strategies to the table. Here's an easy routine for introducing the task cards to your students for the very first time.

1. Discuss and review making inferences in nonfiction and fiction works. **TIP:** Discuss and share some or all of the Comprehension Helper Cards on pages 9–15.

2. Display an enlarged version of a task card using an interactive whiteboard, document camera, or overhead projector.

3. Cover the mini-passage and display just the title. Read it aloud and invite students to predict what the informational article or literary passage will be about.

4. Read the mini-passage aloud, slowly and clearly.

5. Boost fluency by inviting a student volunteer to read the mini-passage again using his or her best "performance" voice.

6. Discuss the mini-passage. Encourage students to comment and connect it to other texts as well as to their own lives.

7. Call attention to the five key questions to the right of the mini-passage. Explain that the first two are related to making inferences. Model how to properly "mine" the passage for clues to help students make sound inferences. Demonstrate how to cite text evidence and paraphrase it to respond to question 2. **TIP:** Use a highlighter to mark clues in the passage.

8. Challenge students to respond thoughtfully to each question.

9. Number and record each answer on chart paper. Model using complete sentences with proper spelling and punctuation.

10. Give your class a round of applause for successfully completing a task card. Now they're ready to tackle the cards independently.

INTEGRATING THE TASK CARDS INTO THE CLASSROOM

The task cards can be used in many ways. Here are 10 quick ideas to maximize learning:

- Challenge students to complete one task card every morning.

- Invite partners to read the task cards together and respond in writing.

- Invite small groups to read, discuss, and respond to the task cards orally.

- Place the task cards in a learning center for students to complete independently.

- Carve out time to do a task card with the whole class a few times a week.

- Encourage individual students to build fluency by reading a task card aloud to the class. They can then solicit answers from fellow students.

- Laminate the task cards and place them in a recipe box for students to do after they've completed the rest of their work.

- Send the task cards home for students to complete with or without parental help.

- Provide students with designated notebooks for recording the answers to all of the task cards.

- Create a class chart, telling students to make a check mark each time they complete a task card. The first student to reach 100 wins a prize!

COMPREHENSION HELPER

Inference

A conclusion about a text based on clues within it.

TIP Text clues are words or details that help you figure out an unstated idea. To make an inference, combine clues in the text with your own background knowledge to figure out what the author is *really* trying to tell you.

Informational Examples

- *If a nonfiction book says, "Harriet Tubman walked through the dangerous, dark woods all by herself," you could **infer** that she was very brave.*
- *If an article states, "Sugar tastes sweet, but can have sour consequences," you could **infer** that eating too much sugar is bad for your health.*

Literary Examples

- *If a fiction book says, "Carlos had very sweaty palms," you could **infer** that he was nervous.*
- *If a fiction story states, "Ashley got chills and began to cough," you could **infer** that she was getting sick.*

COMPREHENSION HELPER

Text Evidence

Words, phrases, or sentences in a text that provide information, answer a question, or support a claim.

TIP When citing text you can frame your text evidence with a sentence stem, such as *The passage says* or *According to the text*. Follow that with a comma or colon (, or :). Then, place the exact words from the text inside the quotation marks. (See examples on the right.) Another option is to *paraphrase*, or restate, the text evidence in your own words.

Informational Examples

- *The passage says, "Grizzly bears usually emerge from hibernation in early spring."*
- *According to the text: "Medieval castles ranged from simple wood structures to massive stone compounds."*

Literary Examples

- *The story says, "Lydia's bedroom was neat and orderly, much like her brain."*
- *An example of a simile in the story is: "Today, Jamal felt as free as a bird."*

Context Clues

Hints readers use to figure out the meaning of an unknown word in a text. Context clues can come before or after the unknown word.

TIP Authors use many words you may not know. But nearby words, phrases, and sentences may offer important clues to the unfamiliar word's definition. As you read, play detective and search for clues to the mystery word's meaning. This will help you improve your understanding and your vocabulary without reaching for a dictionary.

Examples

- **Definition Clues:** *The unknown word is defined in the text.*
- **Example Clues:** *An example of the unknown word is provided in the text.*
- **Synonym Clues:** *A word with a similar meaning is near the unknown word.*
- **Antonym Clues:** *A word with the opposite meaning is near the unknown word.*

Main Idea and Details

MAIN IDEA: The big idea, or main point, of a text. The main idea answers this question: *What* is the piece of writing about?

DETAILS: Facts, statements, descriptions, and other information that tell more about the main idea.

TIP Think of the main idea as a big umbrella that "covers" all the smaller details. The main idea of an informational text is often stated as a topic sentence, which can appear anywhere in the text. Be on the lookout for it!

Examples

- **Main Idea:** *Wolves are fascinating mammals.*
- **Detail:** *Wolves live in packs.*

- **Main Idea:** *New York City is a large, diverse city.*
- **Detail:** *Eight million people live in New York City.*

- **Main Idea:** *There are eight planets in our solar system.*
- **Detail:** *The largest planet is Jupiter.*

- **Main Idea:** *Abraham Lincoln was a great president.*
- **Detail:** *Lincoln wrote the Gettysburg Address.*

Compare and Contrast

COMPARE: To look closely at two or more things (people, animals, places, objects, concepts, etc.) to see how they are similar.

CONTRAST: To look closely at two or more things to see how they are different.

TIP To compare and contrast elements of a text, be on the lookout for signal words. *Both, in common, as well as, too,* and *also* relate to similarities. *Differ, however, only, but, while,* and *on the other hand* relate to differences.

Examples

- **Compare:** *Michael Jordan and Larry Bird were both basketball players.*
- **Contrast:** *Jordan played for the Chicago Bulls, while Bird played for the Boston Celtics.*

- **Compare:** *Squirrels and mice are both rodents.*
- **Contrast:** *Squirrels have big, bushy tails. Mice, however, have long, thin tails.*

- **Compare:** *Squares are shapes. Triangles are shapes, too.*
- **Contrast:** *Squares have four sides, but triangles have only three sides.*

Sequence of Events

EVENTS: Important things that happen in a text.

SEQUENCE: The order in which those things happen.

TIP When reading informational text, it is very important to understand the sequence of events. Signal words provide clues that help clarify the order of events. Examples include *first, second, then, next, before, after that, later, last,* and *finally,* as well as specific dates and times.

Example

- **Sequence of events for making a pizza:** *First, you roll out the dough. Second, you ladle on the tomato sauce. Then, you sprinkle on the cheese. Next, you put on the pepperoni. After that, you put on the mushrooms. Last, you bake it in the oven.*

Summarize

Create a brief statement about a text using only the most important details.

TIP When writing a summary, think about how to retell the key ideas of a passage in your own words. Challenge yourself to be short and clear *and* to leave out all the unimportant details.

Example

- **Sample Text:** *Cats make excellent pets. From Nepal to New York, cats are the world's favorite pet! Cats are mammals like bears and bats. The difference is that most cats are gentle and enjoy living with people. There are more than 70 breeds of cats. Cats are fairly easy to care for. They don't need to be walked several times a day like dogs. Plus, they love to sleep. In fact, some cats sleep up to 20 hours a day.*

- **Summary of Text:** *Cats make excellent pets for people all over the world. There are more than 70 different breeds of this gentle mammal. Cats are easy to care for.*

Character

One of the individuals in a story. Characters are usually people, but they can also be animals or even humanized objects.

TIP To better understand characters, read for details that describe them. What makes them unique? Think about what they say and do. Think about how others treat them. Think about how they are like characters in other books or like people you know. Note how they change from the first page to the last.

Examples

- *Harry Potter*
- *Percy Jackson*
- *Mary Poppins*
- *Oliver Twist*
- *Willy Wonka*
- *The Little Engine That Could*
- *Little Red Riding Hood*
- *The Big Bad Wolf*

- *The Cat in the Hat*
- *Curious George*
- *Pa Ingalls*
- *Bambi*
- *Bilbo Baggins*
- *Katniss Everdeen*
- *Greg Heffley*
- *Harriet the Spy*
- *Icarus*

Setting

The place and time in which a story happens. Settings can be realistic or fantastical. Stories can happen in the past, present, or future.

TIP To better understand a setting, read for details that tell where and when the story is happening. Compare the setting to places in your own life as well as to similar locations in other books and movies. When reading, try to form a picture in your mind so you can better "see" where and when the action occurs.

Examples

- *haunted house*
- *kid's bedroom*
- *ancient Greece*
- *New York City*
- *magic forest*
- *under the sea*
- *tree house*
- *Hogwarts*
- *rabbit hole*

- *school*
- *Mars*
- *Alaska*
- *playground*
- *space station*
- *diner*
- *Western town*
- *zoo*
- *log cabin*

Tone

The way the narrator feels about the events, settings, and characters in a story. Tone can reveal a variety of emotions.

TIP Tone is conveyed through every part of a story, including writing style, word choice, and dialogue. The best way to figure out a story's tone is to ask: *What is the narrator's attitude toward the topic, characters, and events?* The narrator's attitude sets the story's tone.

Examples

- *gloomy*
- *fantastical*
- *bossy*
- *annoyed*
- *stuck-up*
- *wise*
- *confused*
- *nervous*
- *dangerous*
- *shady*
- *warmhearted*
- *funny*
- *playful*
- *tired*
- *sincere*

- *zany*
- *enthusiastic*
- *cynical*
- *scared*
- *jealous*
- *disorganized*
- *bored*
- *shy*
- *sarcastic*
- *lonely*
- *joyful*
- *mean*
- *pretentious*
- *angry*
- *witty*

Theme

The big idea or message of a story. A theme is conveyed by title, setting, and symbols. It can also be conveyed by how its characters act, learn, and change.

TIP To figure out a theme, read the whole story and ask: *How did it end? What was the author trying to tell me? How did the main characters change? What did they learn? What did I learn?* Put all your answers together. Then craft a short sentence, like the ones on the right, that clearly states the theme.

Examples

- *Be true to your own values.*
- *Family loyalty is very important.*
- *Appearances can be deceptive.*
- *Hard work builds character.*
- *Courage comes from facing down fears.*
- *True friends stick together when times get tough.*
- *Differences make people special.*
- *Happiness is contagious.*
- *Cooperation is the key to getting things done.*

Prediction

Using what you know from the text to make a smart guess about what will happen later on in a story.

TIP When you read a story, pause and play detective. Collect clues in the text and use them to make smart guesses about what will happen next. Making predictions keeps you actively engaged with the text and improves your comprehension.

Examples

- *I know that the castle is haunted, so I **predict** the main character will see a ghost.*
- *I know the wolf blew down the straw house, so I **predict** he will blow down the stick house, too.*
- *I know the main character is lonely, so I **predict** she will try to find a friend.*
- *I know the frog was a prince, so I **predict** he will turn back into a prince.*
- *I know the story takes place in a circus, so I **predict** it will be funny.*

100 MAKING INFERENCES TASK CARDS

A Sport Is Born

James Naismith was a gym teacher in Massachusetts. He noticed that there weren't many games to play outside during the cold winters. That seemed to make students become cranky. So in 1891, he invented an indoor game for chilly weather. The goal of his new game was to toss a ball into a peach basket. Naismith nailed two peach baskets high on the wall of the gym. Students loved this new game! Soon, Americans everywhere were playing. Over time, Naismith's game **evolved**, adding new rules. Today, the game he invented is one of the world's most popular sports.

KEY QUESTIONS

1. INFERENCE: What game did James Naismith invent?

2. TEXT EVIDENCE: How do you know? What clues did you find in the text?

3. SUMMARIZE: Summarize the passage in a few sentences.

4. CONTEXT CLUES: What do you think *evolved* means?

☐ changed and grew
☐ stayed the same
☐ became electronic

5. S-T-R-E-T-C-H: Invent a sport. Describe and name it.

The Missing Mona Lisa

The most famous painting in the world is named the *Mona Lisa*. The picture, of a dark-haired woman with a sly smile, was painted in 1506 by Leonardo da Vinci. It hangs in a museum in France. But the *Mona Lisa* didn't get international attention until someone had a sneaky plan in 1911. That year, a man went to the museum, and at closing time he hid. Late that night, he took the *Mona Lisa* off the wall and snuck out of the museum with it. Newspapers everywhere wrote about the

 theft. People were shocked and **outraged**. Fortunately, police ultimately caught the thief and returned the painting to the museum.

KEY QUESTIONS

1. INFERENCE: Was the *Mona Lisa* world-famous in the 1600s?

2. TEXT EVIDENCE: How do you know? What clues did you find in the text?

3. DETAILS: Give one detail about the *Mona Lisa*.

4. CONTEXT CLUES: What do you think *outraged* means?

☐ silly
☐ angry
☐ tired

5. S-T-R-E-T-C-H: What is your favorite work of art? Tell about it.

Bugs, Bugs, Bugs!

How much does a ladybug weigh? Or an ant? Not very much. In fact, if an ant or a ladybug was crawling on your arm, you might not even feel it. Most insects weigh much less than a single ounce. Even the heaviest insect in the world—the goliath beetle—weighs a **measly** 2.5 ounces. That's a little more than a tennis ball. In comparison, you or your best friend weigh about a thousand times that much—and you've not even finished growing. But here's an astonishing fact: If you weighed all the insects on the planet, they would weigh MORE than all the people. Really!

KEY QUESTIONS

1. INFERENCE: Are there more people or insects in the world?

2. TEXT EVIDENCE: How do you know? What clues did you find in the text?

3. MAIN IDEA: What is the main idea of this passage?

4. CONTEXT CLUES: What do you think *measly* means?

☐ humorous
☐ scary
☐ very small

5. S-T-R-E-T-C-H: Were you surprised by what you learned in this passage? Tell why.

I'll Have a Scoop

We call it ice cream. In Italy, they call it gelato. But no matter what name you give it, most people love a dish or a cone filled with this cold dessert. The first president of the United States, George Washington, is said to have been a fan. And so was Thomas Jefferson, our country's third leader. No one is sure when ice cream was first invented, but some **historians** think it has been around for as long as 4,000 years! Way back then, it might have been made from snow flavored with honey or fruit. One thing is certain: On a hot day, this sweet treat certainly hits the spot!

KEY QUESTIONS

1. INFERENCE: Is ice cream only available in the United States?

2. TEXT EVIDENCE: How do you know? What clues did you find in the text?

3. SUMMARIZE: Summarize this passage.

4. CONTEXT CLUES: What do you think *historians* means?

☐ people who like ice cream
☐ people who study the past
☐ people who make gelato

5. S-T-R-E-T-C-H: Describe another food without naming it. See if a partner can figure out what it is.

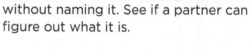

What's in a (Street) Name?

The most **ubiquitous** street names in America are the first five numbers, in that order. That means First Street is the most common street name for U.S. cities. Fifth Street comes in at number five. Also among the top 20 most popular street names are five different trees: Oak, Pine, Maple, Cedar, and Elm. Do you know of any Oak or Elm Streets? Of course, many cities have a Main Street. Main Street is the seventh most popular U.S. street name. Our country has 7,644 Main Streets.

Hill Street comes in as the 20th most popular U.S. street name. There are 4,877 Hill Streets in the United States.

KEY QUESTIONS

1. INFERENCE: If you visited a U.S. city, how likely is it that there would be a Main Street?

2. TEXT EVIDENCE: How do you know? What clues did you find in the text?

3. DETAILS: List these three street names in order of popularity: Main Street, First Street, Hill Street.

4. CONTEXT CLUES: What do you think *ubiquitous* means?

☐ rarely used
☐ unknown
☐ widely used

5. S-T-R-E-T-C-H: Write directions to a favorite place, using street names.

Bright Inventions

What do you think the very earliest human beings did when the sun went down? Well, they probably just sat around in the dark. To have light at night, people had to learn how to use fire. Over time, humans found new ways to create light at night. Ancient Romans get credit for making the first candles. During the 1800s, people began to use gas to light up their houses. Then, along came Thomas Alva Edison. In 1878, he figured out how to use electricity to **generate** light. Thank you, Thomas Alva Edison!

KEY QUESTIONS

1. INFERENCE: What invention is credited to Thomas Edison?

2. TEXT EVIDENCE: How do you know? What clues did you find in the text?

3. SEQUENCE OF EVENTS: List these light-generating inventions in the order they came to be: electric light, fire light, candle light, gas light.

4. CONTEXT CLUES: What do you think *generate* means?

☐ shade
☐ flash
☐ make

5. S-T-R-E-T-C-H: Are you glad electric lights were invented? Tell why.

INFERENCE: INFORMATIONAL

Saving the Manatee

Over the last century, many species have become endangered including the Florida manatee. This large, gray mammal lives in the oceans near Florida. As the state became more populated, the number of manatees decreased until there were only a few thousand left. A main problem was fast-moving boats, which hit and killed these gentle creatures. In 1967, however, some people began to take action. They worked hard to get manatees put on the endangered species list. This list caused the government to create "protection zones" to get boats to slow down in manatee **habitats**. The outcome: This remarkable mammal was taken off the endangered species list in 2017.

KEY QUESTIONS

1. INFERENCE: Is the number of manatees still decreasing?

2. TEXT EVIDENCE: How do you know? What clues did you find in the text?

3. SUMMARIZE: Summarize this passage.

4. CONTEXT CLUES: What do you think *habitats* means?

- [ ] homes
- [ ] boats
- [ ] cows

5. S-T-R-E-T-C-H: Do you think it is important to protect endangered species? Why?

INFERENCE: INFORMATIONAL

Distance From the Sun

The eight planets in our solar system are Mercury, Venus, Earth, Mars, Jupiter, Saturn, Uranus, and Neptune. They are listed in order of their distance from the sun. Mercury is closest to the sun. For that reason, it is very hot. The average temperature on Mercury is 869 degrees Fahrenheit! Humans could never **dwell** on such a hot planet. Next is Venus. Venus is also extremely hot, with an average temperature of 860 degrees. Earth is the third from the sun, and luckily, things are a lot cooler here. Earth's average temperature is a comfy 57 degrees. As planets get farther from the sun, they get colder and colder.

KEY QUESTIONS

1. INFERENCE: Is Neptune hot or cold?

2. TEXT EVIDENCE: How do you know? What clues did you find in the text?

3. MAIN IDEA: What is the main idea of this passage?

4. CONTEXT CLUES: What do you think *dwell* means?

- [ ] leave
- [ ] study
- [ ] live

5. S-T-R-E-T-C-H: Is Jupiter hotter or colder than Earth? How do you know?

INFERENCE: INFORMATIONAL

Ye Olde Measurements

There are many old-fashioned measurements that aren't used much anymore. For example, a league measures distance while traveling in the ocean. One league equals about three and a half miles. A candela is a measurement of brightness. A 40,000-candela light would be blindingly bright. Then there is stone, an old English measurement of weight. English people used to and sometimes still do, say things like, "He's a healthy young lad. Weighs three stone, he does." What would happen if you tried to pick up a barbell that weighed 10 stone? You'd probably **strain** and sweat. And the barbell probably wouldn't budge at all!

KEY QUESTIONS

1. INFERENCE: Would you describe a barbell that weighs 10 stone as light or heavy?

2. TEXT EVIDENCE: How do you know? What clues did you find in the text?

3. INFERENCE: Candela is an old-fashioned measurement of brightness. What bright object do you think its name is based on?

4. CONTEXT CLUES: What do you think *strain* means?

☐ make great effort ☐ become lazy
☐ lift weights

5. S-T-R-E-T-C-H: A stone equals 14 pounds. Convert the following into pounds: a one-stone puppy, a four-stone boy, a 20-stone refrigerator.

INFERENCE: INFORMATIONAL

About Albert Einstein

Albert Einstein is one of the most famous scientists who ever lived. You've probably seen pictures of him, with his wild mop of messy white hair. Einstein was born in Germany in 1879. He later moved to the United States, where he lived until his death in 1955. He was a physicist—a scientist who studies the universe and how it works. Some of Einstein's ideas and theories completely changed the way people think about the **cosmos**. In 1921, he won the Nobel Prize in Physics. The Nobel Prize is the most important award a scientist can get.

KEY QUESTIONS

1. INFERENCE: Was Einstein an important scientist?

2. TEXT EVIDENCE: How do you know? What clues did you find in the text?

3. MAIN IDEA: What is the main idea of this passage?

4. CONTEXT CLUES: What do you think *cosmos* means?

☐ universe
☐ Germany
☐ hair

5. S-T-R-E-T-C-H: A physicist is a kind of scientist. Name another kind of scientist and tell what you know about his or her job.

INFERENCE: INFORMATIONAL

Chimps Like Us

Jane Goodall is a scientist who studied chimpanzees in Africa. She didn't just study them for a few weeks or months. She studied them for many years. She **relocated** to Africa and lived in forests among the chimpanzees. She watched what they did and how they acted. What she discovered changed a lot of people's minds about the differences between humans and animals. She discovered that chimps use tools. They communicate with one

another and sometimes disagree. They have leaders. They even hug and kiss each other and pat each other on the back.

KEY QUESTIONS

1. INFERENCE: Are chimps similar to humans in some ways?

2. TEXT EVIDENCE: How do you know? What clues did you find in the text?

3. COMPARE AND CONTRAST: What are some ways chimps and humans are different?

4. CONTEXT CLUES: What do you think *relocated* means?

☐ swam
☐ studied
☐ moved

5. S-T-R-E-T-C-H: Can you think of some other ways humans and animals are similar?

INFERENCE: INFORMATIONAL

A Spoonful a Day

Maybe you start your day by taking a vitamin. In the old days, many kids started their day with a spoonful of cod liver oil. This thick liquid, usually brown or dark yellow in color, comes from a fish called a cod. It contains vitamins A and D and many other healthy **ingredients**. "It's good for you, sweetie," mothers used to say, offering a spoonful. Kids everywhere had the same reaction: shaking their heads, scrunching up their faces, and shutting their mouths super-tight.

KEY QUESTIONS

1. INFERENCE: How do you think cod liver oil tastes?

2. TEXT EVIDENCE: How do you know? What clues did you find in the text?

3. MAIN IDEA: Describe the main idea of this passage in a sentence or two.

4. CONTEXT CLUES: What do you think *ingredients* means?

☐ liquids
☐ foods
☐ parts that make up it

5. S-T-R-E-T-C-H: Create an imaginary, old-fashioned advertising jingle to convince kids to take their cod liver oil.

Surprising Snakes

Snakes are a kind of reptile. They are related to other reptiles such as lizards and turtles. Snakes have **unique** skin. From time to time, they shed their skin. Sometimes it comes off in one long, dry piece. That piece might even include the two little protective scales that cover a snake's eyes. Beneath the snake's old skin is a brand-new one. A snake's skin may be so shiny that you might expect it to be damp and slimy. In fact, it's the opposite. Yes, snakes are full of surprises!

KEY QUESTIONS

1. INFERENCE: How would a snake's skin feel to the touch?

2. TEXT EVIDENCE: How do you know? What clues did you find in the text?

3. SUMMARIZE: Summarize this passage in a few sentences.

4. CONTEXT CLUES: What do you think *unique* means?

☐ scaled
☐ one of a kind
☐ slippery

5. S-T-R-E-T-C-H: Choose an animal or object. Describe how it feels to the touch.

Watery Venice

If you were to visit the city of Venice in Italy, you would notice some things that are pretty unusual. First of all, Venice is filled with water. In fact, the city is actually made up of 118 small islands that are separated by **narrow** waterways. These waterways are known as canals, and some of them are really skinny, less than the width of a city street. Another thing you'd notice is that there are no cars. In fact, cars aren't even allowed. Instead, people get where they're going by walking or by riding in long, thin boats known as gondolas.

KEY QUESTIONS

1. INFERENCE: Do people who live in Venice need a driver's license to get around?

2. TEXT EVIDENCE: How do you know? What clues did you find in the text?

3. COMPARE AND CONTRAST: How is Venice different from most cities?

4. CONTEXT CLUES: What do you think *narrow* means?

☐ wide
☐ watery
☐ thin

5. S-T-R-E-T-C-H: There are more than 300 bridges in Venice. Why do you think there are so many?

A Very Rare Cat

A liger is a real animal. Its name is a **melding** of the names of two very big cats. Ligers have yellowish fur. They also have stripes. A full-grown liger can be 10 feet long from its nose to the tip of its tail. A liger named Hercules set the world record for being the heaviest cat. Hercules weighed 922 pounds. That's one big kitty! Fortunately, ligers aren't house pets. They aren't found in nature, either. In fact, ligers are very rare. There are probably fewer than 100 in the entire world. The only place you might see a liger is at a zoo.

KEY QUESTIONS

1. INFERENCE: A liger is a mix of what two kinds of cats?

2. TEXT EVIDENCE: How do you know? What clues did you find in the text?

3. DETAILS: How much did the heaviest cat in the world weigh?

4. CONTEXT CLUES: What do you think *melding* means?

☐ confusing
☐ erasing
☐ combining

5. S-T-R-E-T-C-H: Dream up an imaginary animal mix. What would you call it? Describe this creature.

Freshwater, Please!

Imagine two people in a boat out at sea. Now imagine they run out of water. They'd grow thirstier and thirstier. They would be surrounded by a **vast** supply of water, and yet they shouldn't drink a single drop. That's because the ocean's water is too salty for humans—and most animals—to drink. Not only does it taste really bad, but our bodies just can't process all that salt. So even if we drink it, it doesn't nourish our tissues the way *freshwater*—water without salt—does. In fact, drinking salt water just makes people thirstier, and sick, too. There are ways to remove the salt from water, but it's not easy to do. So for now, people have to rely on freshwater.

KEY QUESTIONS

1. INFERENCE: Can humans survive by drinking only seawater?

2. TEXT EVIDENCE: How do you know? What clues did you find in the text?

3. MAIN IDEA: What is the main idea of this passage?

4. CONTEXT CLUES: What do you think *vast* means?

☐ huge
☐ strange
☐ thirsty

5. S-T-R-E-T-C-H: To stay safe in a boat at sea, what are smart things to bring along?

Steps on the Moon

The first astronauts went to the moon in 1969. It took Neil Armstrong, Buzz Aldrin, and Michael Collins five days to get to the moon on the Apollo 11 spaceflight. Collins stayed inside the ship, but Armstrong and Aldrin, wearing special space suits, **ventured** out of their spacecraft and walked on the moon. The moon's ground was rocky, and it was covered with a layer of sandy dust. As they walked, the astronaut's boots left big footprints. Unlike Earth, there is no air or wind or rain or snow on the moon. So 50 years later, the footprints left by the astronauts are still there, just as they were that day.

KEY QUESTIONS

1. INFERENCE: Do you think people could live on the moon right now?

2. TEXT EVIDENCE: How do you know? What clues did you find in the text?

3. COMPARE AND CONTRAST: How is the moon different from Earth?

4. CONTEXT CLUES: What do you think *ventured* means?

☐ waited
☐ traveled
☐ covered

5. S-T-R-E-T-C-H: If you walked on a dusty path on Earth, would your footprints still be there a year later? Why or why not?

What Is Wikipedia?

The website Wikipedia was started in 2001. It has the perfect name. Wikipedia is a mix of encyclopedia and *wiki*, which means "quick" in a native Hawaiian language. What makes Wikipedia special is that it's created by the **public**. Say, for example, that there was an exciting new boy band. Anybody could start a Wikipedia page for them. What if that band had a number-one song? Anyone could add this piece of information to that same Wikipedia page. People everywhere go online to help with Wikipedia. The world's citizens have created 40 million different Wikipedia topic pages in 301 different languages.

KEY QUESTIONS

1. INFERENCE: Could a 10-year-old girl create a Wikipedia page for her favorite author?

2. TEXT EVIDENCE: How do you know? What clues did you find in the text?

3. INFERENCE: Could the girl's 8-year-old brother add new information about the author?

4. CONTEXT CLUES: What do you think *public* means?

☐ famous celebrities
☐ people in the community
☐ trained writers

5. S-T-R-E-T-C-H: Imagine you created a Wikipedia page. What would the topic be? Write a paragraph about it.

Electric Cars

Until recently, all cars ran on gas or similar fuel. But today, cars that use electricity are becoming popular. Some cars run on both electricity *and* gas. These are known as hybrids. Other cars run on electricity alone. Electric cars and hybrids are **beneficial** for the environment because they use less fuel. But today's electric cars are not the first ones ever made. In 1891, a scientist in Iowa named William Morrison built the first electric car. In 1899, Thomas Edison began working on a very large battery that would power cars, but he gave up on the idea. Eventually, cars that ran on gas became the standard.

KEY QUESTIONS

1. INFERENCE: Why are electric and hybrid cars becoming more popular?

2. TEXT EVIDENCE: How do you know? What clues did you find in the text?

3. SUMMARIZE: Summarize this passage.

4. CONTEXT CLUES: What do you think *beneficial* means?

☐ harmful
☐ helpful
☐ new

5. S-T-R-E-T-C-H: What are some other ways we use electricity? Make a list.

A Hare or a Rabbit?

Have you ever heard of a hare? If so, you might think it's another name for a rabbit. That's what many people think. But while they look similar, hares and rabbits are different animals. Rabbits are born without fur and with their eyes shut. It takes them awhile to see. Hares, on the other hand, are born with fur and can see right away. Adult hares are usually bigger than rabbits, with larger ears. Hares also live above ground. Most rabbits make their nests underground in **burrows**. Lastly, rabbits are gentle and enjoy time with others. Hares are wild, fast-running, and prefer to spend time alone.

KEY QUESTIONS

1. INFERENCE: Which would make a better pet, a rabbit or a hare?

2. TEXT EVIDENCE: How do you know? What clues did you find in the text?

3. MAIN IDEA: What is the main idea of this passage?

4. CONTEXT CLUES: What do you think *burrows* means?

☐ ears
☐ snakes
☐ tunnels

5. S-T-R-E-T-C-H: Can you think of two other animals that are similar but different? Write about them.

Visiting the Vessel

New York City's big attractions get huge numbers of visitors. The Statue of Liberty opened to the public in 1886. It still gets 4.5 million visitors a year. In 2009, the High Line park opened in New York City. It gets 5 million visitors a year. In 2019, New York City opened a new **attraction**. It's called the Vessel and people are very excited about it. The Vessel is 16 stories tall. It has 154 flights of stairs, and 2,500 steps in all. Visitors can move all over the Vessel by using its many walkways and stairs. They can climb to the very top for an amazing view. Would you like to visit the Vessel in New York City?

KEY QUESTIONS

1. INFERENCE: Is the Vessel likely to get a small or large number of visitors?

2. TEXT EVIDENCE: How do you know? What clues did you find in the text?

3. COMPARE AND CONTRAST: Which New York City attraction is older, the Statue of Liberty or the High Line? Which gets more visitors?

4. CONTEXT CLUES: What do you think *attraction* means?

☐ large suitcase
☐ round building
☐ exciting place to visit

5. S-T-R-E-T-C-H: Describe a favorite attraction in your community.

Animal Symbols

Many countries around the world include animals in their national symbols. They usually choose animals that can be found in that country. For example, Peru's national symbol is the vicuña. Vicuñas, which are closely related to llamas, live high in the Andes Mountains of Peru. South Africa's symbol is the antelope. That makes sense. Antelopes can be seen prancing in the savannas of South Africa. Australia chose two animals for its symbol. Can you guess which ones? The kangaroo and the emu. Of course, America's symbol is the bald eagle. Bald eagles are powerful, beautiful, and **majestic** creatures.

KEY QUESTIONS

1. INFERENCE: Do bald eagles live in the United States?

2. TEXT EVIDENCE: How do you know? What clues did you find in the text?

3. DETAILS: Give two details about vicuñas.

4. CONTEXT CLUES: What do you think *majestic* means?

☐ tiny
☐ amazing
☐ flightless

5. S-T-R-E-T-C-H: Invent a symbol. What is it a symbol of? Why?

It's Hot in Here

The temperature inside a person's body is right around 98.6 degrees Fahrenheit. That is, unless the person gets sick. Then things can really heat up, and the person develops a fever. With a fever, a person's temperature might rise as high as 103 degrees, or even higher. But why? The flu and similar illnesses are caused by invading viruses and bacteria. A higher temperature helps our bodies fight and beat back these bugs. A higher temperature is also less **hospitable** for the germs and can make them weaker. Eventually our body wins the battle, and we're healthy again.

KEY QUESTIONS

1. INFERENCE: Is having a fever good or bad when you're sick?

2. TEXT EVIDENCE: How do you know? What clues did you find in the text?

3. MAIN IDEA: What is the main idea of this passage?

4. CONTEXT CLUES: What do you think *hospitable* means?

☐ friendly
☐ sick
☐ hot

5. S-T-R-E-T-C-H: Have you ever had a fever? Tell about it.

Paul, the Celebrity Octopus

In 2010, an octopus showed a strange talent for predicting soccer match winners. His name was Paul, and he lived in an aquarium in Germany. Before big matches, Paul's food would be placed in two different boxes. One box had a picture of the German soccer team's flag. The other box had a picture of the **rival** team's flag. Whatever box Paul ate from was taken as his prediction of the winning team. Incredibly, he got it right for all seven of Germany's World Cup matches. There were many news stories about Paul, and he became a world-famous octopus.

KEY QUESTIONS

1. INFERENCE: When Paul predicted a German team win, what flag was on his food box?

2. TEXT EVIDENCE: How do you know? What clues did you find in the text?

3. DETAILS: How many matches did Germany win in the 2010 World Cup?

4. CONTEXT CLUES: What do you think *rival* means?

☐ squid
☐ friend
☐ competitor

5. S-T-R-E-T-C-H: Do you think Paul really knew who was going to win or just got lucky? Tell why you think so.

Grapes and Raisins

Grapes and raisins seem like two completely different fruits, but they're actually the same. How is that possible? A grape is fresh, and a raisin is dried. That's the only difference. Think about biting into a nice, plump grape. It's juicy because there's a lot of water inside. Raisins are made when grapes are dried in the sun. Over time, the sun's heat causes the water in the grape to leave, or **evaporate**. What's left is a smaller, wrinkled, dried-up piece of fruit. Raisins are sweeter than grapes, too. That's because when the water dries up, what's left is lots of sugar.

KEY QUESTIONS

1. INFERENCE: Which would you use to make juice, a grape or a raisin?

2. TEXT EVIDENCE: How do you know? What clues did you find in the text?

3. COMPARE AND CONTRAST: Tell one way that grapes and raisins are similar and one way they're different.

4. CONTEXT CLUES: What do you think *evaporate* means?

☐ become larger
☐ turn from liquid to vapor
☐ become smaller

5. S-T-R-E-T-C-H: Would you rather eat some grapes or some raisins? Tell why.

Birds of a Feather

What makes a bird a bird? It's not wings. Many creatures have wings but are not birds. For example, dragonflies and bees have wings. They aren't birds, though. They are insects. Laying eggs doesn't make a bird a bird, either. Many creatures lay eggs but are not birds. For example, lizards and turtles lay eggs. They aren't birds, though. They are reptiles. So what makes a bird a bird? Here's the answer: Birds have feathers. No other creatures have this **characteristic**. In fact, some types of birds can't even fly. They're still birds, though, because they have fabulous feathers!

KEY QUESTIONS

1. INFERENCE: An ostrich has feathers, but can't fly. What kind of creature is it?

2. TEXT EVIDENCE: How do you know? What clues did you find in the text?

3. MAIN IDEA: What is the main idea of this passage?

4. CONTEXT CLUES: What do you think *characteristic* means?

☐ color
☐ animal
☐ specific feature

5. S-T-R-E-T-C-H: How many different types of birds can you name? Make a list.

First in Flight

On December 17, 1903, Orville and Wilbur Wright made history. The brothers were on a beach at a place called Kitty Hawk. They flew an airplane for 59 seconds. The plane traveled 852 feet. It was a short flight that lasted for a brief **duration**. Still, the Wright brothers deserve credit for the first successful airplane flight. Today, jet planes travel thousands of miles and remain in the air for many hours. But the Wright brothers' famous flight is still remembered. In fact, license plates on cars in North Carolina have the slogan "First in Flight."

KEY QUESTIONS

1. INFERENCE: What state is Kitty Hawk in?

2. TEXT EVIDENCE: How do you know? What clues did you find in the text?

3. DETAILS: How long did the Wright brothers' flight last? How far did the plane travel?

4. CONTEXT CLUES: What do you think *duration* means?

☐ amount of time
☐ distance
☐ speed measurement

5. S-T-R-E-T-C-H: What slogan would you put on your state's license plate? Why?

Dual Language

If you were riding in a car in Canada and came to a stop sign, you would see the familiar bright red sign. But on it would be two words instead of one: *Stop* and *Arrêt*. In Canada, many signs are written in both English and French. And both English and French are the country's official languages. The reason for this is that many of Canada's earliest settlers were from France. Today, in most parts of Canada, most people speak English. But in one **region** of the country, the province of Quebec, French is the primary language that people speak.

S T O P
ARRÊT

KEY QUESTIONS

1. INFERENCE: What does *Arrêt* mean in English?

2. TEXT EVIDENCE: How do you know? What clues did you find in the text?

3. COMPARE AND CONTRAST: How are the signs different in Canada than they are in the United States?

4. CONTEXT CLUES: What do you think *region* means?

☐ language
☐ sign
☐ section

5. S-T-R-E-T-C-H: Would you like to learn a new language? Which one and why?

A Towering Achievement

It's one of the most famous creations in the world. It's also one of the most unusual. And even if you've never been to Paris, France, you've probably seen pictures of it. What is it? The Eiffel Tower. The Eiffel Tower was built by Gustave Eiffel in 1889. This very tall tower is 984 feet high. It has 108 stories, with 1,710 steps. But visitors are only permitted to walk part of the way. An elevator **ushers** people up to the top. At night the tower shines brightly, lit by 20,000 light bulbs! Millions of people visit the Eiffel Tower every year.

KEY QUESTIONS

1. INFERENCE: Is the Eiffel Tower popular with sightseers?

2. TEXT EVIDENCE: How do you know? What clues did you find in the text?

3. DETAILS: How many stories and steps does the Eiffel Tower have?

4. CONTEXT CLUES: What do you think *ushers* means?

☐ guides
☐ rises
☐ shines

5. S-T-R-E-T-C-H: The Eiffel Tower is named after the man who created it. Think of another name for the tower. Why did you choose it?

Bobbie the Wonder Dog

In 1923, an Oregon family took their dog, Bobbie, on a car trip to Indiana. They were visiting relatives more than 2,500 miles away. When it was time to drive back home, they couldn't find Bobbie anywhere. He had wandered off and got lost. They were heartbroken, and they drove home without him. Nine months later, a dog that looked like Bobbie showed up at their house. The dog was **scrawny** and dirty. His paws were raw and he didn't smell very good. It was Bobbie! He had walked 2,500 miles to get back home! Newspapers wrote about Bobbie, and there was even a movie made about his incredible story.

KEY QUESTIONS

1. INFERENCE: Did Bobbie miss his home and family?

2. TEXT EVIDENCE: How do you know? What clues did you find in the text?

3. DETAILS: How many months did it take Bobbie to return home?

4. CONTEXT CLUES: What do you think *scrawny* means?

☐ tall
☐ beautiful
☐ skinny

5. S-T-R-E-T-C-H: What can you infer about Bobbie's trip home?

Seeing Inside

X-rays were discovered in 1895. Since that time, X-ray machines have been used to see the insides of many different things. X-rays are **versatile**. Doctors use X-rays to see inside a patient's body. An X-ray can show a doctor a person's skeleton or brain. Dentists use X-rays to see inside a patient's teeth. An X-ray can show a dentist if a person has any cavities. X-rays don't only show a person's insides, though. They can also show what's inside a bag, a box, or almost anything at all.

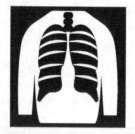

KEY QUESTIONS

1. INFERENCE: If a backpack was filled with marbles, what would an X-ray show?

2. TEXT EVIDENCE: How do you know? What clues did you find in the text?

3. SUMMARIZE: Write a summary of this passage.

4. CONTEXT CLUES: What do you think *versatile* mean?

☐ invisible
☐ useless
☐ useful

5. S-T-R-E-T-C-H: If you could use an X-ray to look inside a cat's body or a clown's suitcase, which would you choose? Why?

Faster Messages

Today, when people want to send greetings to a friend, they have lots of options. They can send a text message or an email, or they can send a card in the mail. But 40 years ago, regular mail was the **primary** way people sent notes. In fact, the technology that allows us to send text messages and emails has only been around for 30 years. It's nice to get a note in the mail, but the downside is that it's slow. Most mail takes a few days to arrive, which is why it's sometimes called "snail mail."

KEY QUESTIONS

1. INFERENCE: Did people send text messages 50 years ago?

2. TEXT EVIDENCE: How do you know? What clues did you find in the text?

3. MAIN IDEA: What is the main idea of this passage?

4. CONTEXT CLUES: What do you think *primary* means?

☐ slow
☐ main
☐ scary

5. S-T-R-E-T-C-H: What is your favorite type of mail? Why?

Painter Pablo Picasso

Pablo Picasso is one of the most famous painters of all time. During his long career as an artist, he tried out many different styles. From 1901 to 1904, he mostly used the color blue in his paintings. He painted blue skies and blue water. He painted rooms with blue walls and blue people. These three years became known as Picasso's Blue Period. Then the **renowned** artist was ready to try something new. For his paintings, he started using shades of light pink, a color also known as rose. This was the beginning of Picasso's Rose Period.

KEY QUESTIONS

1. INFERENCE: During his Rose Period, what color might Picasso have used to paint a person's face?

2. TEXT EVIDENCE: How do you know? What clues did you find in the text?

3. SEQUENCE OF EVENTS: Which came first, Picasso's Blue Period or his Rose Period?

4. CONTEXT CLUES: What do you think *renowned* means?

☐ famous
☐ old
☐ celery-loving

5. S-T-R-E-T-C-H: Imagine Picasso had a Purple Period. Describe one of his paintings from this time.

Great Big States

The three biggest states in order of size are Alaska, Texas, and California. Alaska is so huge you could fit 425 of the smallest state, Rhode Island, inside it. Texas comes next. It is so large that it used to be its own country. That's right: Before Texas became a state in 1845, it was known as the Republic of Texas. California is quite big as well. It has 840 miles of coastline and 420 different beaches. What state comes next? The answer is Montana. Though sizable, you can still fit four Montana's inside Alaska. The state of Alaska is simply **humongous**!

KEY QUESTIONS

1. INFERENCE: Is Rhode Island a big or little state?

2. TEXT EVIDENCE: How do you know? What clues did you find in the text?

3. DETAILS: What is the fourth-largest state? How do you know it's fourth?

4. CONTEXT CLUES: What do you think *humongous* means?

☐ huge
☐ dry
☐ independent

5. S-T-R-E-T-C-H: Which is your favorite of the four biggest states? Why?

Count the Rings!

If a tree falls in the woods, you can figure out its age. How? You can examine its round stump, and count the rings. Many kinds of trees add one growth ring each year. So the stump of a very old tree would have many, many rings. In California, there is a **towering** type of tree called a giant sequoia (pronounced se-coy-a). These trees can grow to great heights. Some stretch more than 300 feet into the air. Giant sequoias can live for a long time. After one fell over, people counted 3,200 rings on its stump. Wow! That was a record number of rings for a giant sequoia.

KEY QUESTIONS

1. INFERENCE: How old was the giant sequoia with 3,200 rings?

2. TEXT EVIDENCE: How do you know? What clues did you find in the text?

3. INFERENCE: If a tree's stump had 25 growth rings, how old would it be?

4. CONTEXT CLUES: What do you think *towering* means?

☐ very weak
☐ very old
☐ very tall

5. S-T-R-E-T-C-H: Do you think it's important to take care of old trees? Write about it.

Unsinkable

The *Titanic* was a giant ocean liner built in 1912. At the time, it was the biggest ship in the world. Its owners said it was unsinkable. But on its first **voyage**, it hit an iceberg, and then it slowly began to sink. People onboard had to get into lifeboats so they wouldn't drown. A woman named Molly Brown was one of the passengers. Instead of quickly getting into a lifeboat herself, she stayed on deck and helped others, making sure they were safe. Later, she helped row a lifeboat on the cold, rough sea. Afterwards, people called her the "Unsinkable Molly Brown."

KEY QUESTIONS

1. INFERENCE: Did Molly survive her trip on the *Titanic*?

2. TEXT EVIDENCE: How do you know? What clues did you find in the text?

3. SUMMARIZE: Summarize this passage.

4. CONTEXT CLUES: What do you think *voyage* means?

☐ trip at sea
☐ room on a boat
☐ day at the dock

5. S-T-R-E-T-C-H: People considered Molly Brown a hero. Do you agree? Why or why not?

A Funny Frog

Have you ever heard of a *paradox*? A paradox is a kind of riddle. It refers to something that is the opposite of what you expect. In South America there is a frog that is known as the "paradoxical" frog. Like many frogs, the paradoxical frog is **nocturnal**, and so it's active at night. It lives in ponds and lakes, and it eats insects. But what makes the paradoxical frog so unusual is that when it's young, it's very big—about 10 inches long. Then as it "grows," it gets smaller! By the time it's an adult frog, it's only about three and a half inches long.

KEY QUESTIONS

1. INFERENCE: Why is this frog called the "paradoxical" frog?

2. TEXT EVIDENCE: How do you know? What clues did you find in the text?

3. DETAILS: Give two more details about the paradoxical frog.

4. CONTEXT CLUES: What do you think *nocturnal* means?

☐ active at night
☐ hungry
☐ a riddle

5. S-T-R-E-T-C-H: Can you think of another paradox? Write about it.

The Metric System

There are two common ways to measure distances. In the imperial system, distance is measured in inches, feet, and miles. In the metric system, common measurements include millimeters, meters, and kilometers. Millimeters are **minuscule**. A pencil point is roughly one millimeter across. Meanwhile, one meter is a much longer distance than one millimeter. If an adult spreads his or her arms, the distance from one hand to the other would be about a meter. One kilometer is an even longer distance. It would take you about 10 minutes to walk one kilometer. How many kilometers do you think you walk in a day?

KEY QUESTIONS

1. INFERENCE: Would five millimeters be a short or a long distance?

2. TEXT EVIDENCE: How do you know? What clues did you find in the text?

3. DETAILS: Which three units of measurement mentioned in this passage are part of the imperial system?

4. CONTEXT CLUES: What do you think *minuscule* means?

☐ huge
☐ tiny
☐ unmeasurable

5. S-T-R-E-T-C-H: Which measurement system do you use most often? What do you measure with it?

Triple Trouble

A common word part is *tri*. It means "three." A triangle, for example, is a shape with three sides. A trilogy is a story that is broken into three separate parts. *The Hunger Games* is a popular trilogy. Another word that uses *tri* is *triathlon*. A triathlon is a race with three **distinct** parts. There's a running part, a biking part, and a swimming part. Would you like to try a triathlon? Sounds like triple trouble! There's another word that uses *tri*.

KEY QUESTIONS

1. INFERENCE: Would "triple trouble" be more trouble than regular trouble?

2. TEXT EVIDENCE: How do you know? What clues did you find in the text?

3. SUMMARIZE: Summarize this passage in a few sentences.

4. CONTEXT CLUES: What do you think *distinct* means?

☐ separate and different
☐ similar
☐ big and angry

5. S-T-R-E-T-C-H: What other *tri* words can you think of? Make a list.

Velkommen to Minnesota!

Norway has an incredible 63,000 miles of coastline. Throughout its history, the ocean has been very important to Norwegians. They like to eat fish, and fishing has always been a favorite job. During the 1800s, large numbers of Norwegians started to **immigrate** to America. One of the main states they moved to was Minnesota. In fact, many Norwegians moved to one particular Minnesota city, Duluth. Duluth sits right on the shore of giant Lake Superior. This was a good choice. It made Norwegians feel right at home in their new country, and it allowed them to do the work they love.

KEY QUESTIONS

1. INFERENCE: What job did many Norwegians do after they moved to Duluth?

2. TEXT EVIDENCE: How do you know? What clues did you find in the text?

3. DETAILS: What do you think *velkommen* means? In what language?

4. CONTEXT CLUES: What do you think *immigrate* means?

☐ fly south in winter
☐ move
☐ cut cheese into small pieces

5. S-T-R-E-T-C-H: What job would you like to do when you grow up? Why?

Meet the Beatles

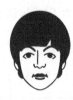

The Beatles are one of the most famous rock bands ever. They are known as the Fab Four. The band was formed in England in 1960. The Beatles had many number-one hit songs, including "Yesterday," "Let It Be," and "Help!" Then, in 1970, the Beatles broke up. The Fab Four went their separate ways. That made fans very sad. But their music has **endured**. It still remains popular. In fact, each day, millions of people around the world listen to the Beatles.

KEY QUESTIONS

1. INFERENCE: How many band members were in the Beatles?

2. TEXT EVIDENCE: How do you know? What clues did you find in the text?

3. SEQUENCE OF EVENTS: What year did the Beatles start as a band? When did they end?

4. CONTEXT CLUES: What do you think *endured* means?

☐ been forgotten
☐ gotten lost
☐ lasted

5. S-T-R-E-T-C-H: Do you have a favorite musical group or type of music? Write about it.

A Long-Ago Long Run

In ancient Greece, a famous battle was fought at a place called Marathon. The Greeks defeated the Persians. A messenger set off with the news. He ran all the way to Athens, where he told the emperor about the Greek **victory**. He was so exhausted that he then fell over and died. The part about the messenger dying is probably a myth. But the battle really happened, although it was long ago. Marathon and Athens really are about 26 miles apart. The tale of the messenger's run would inspire the name of a type of long-distance running race that's very popular nowadays.

KEY QUESTIONS

1. INFERENCE: What popular long-distance race takes its name from an ancient Greek battle?

2. TEXT EVIDENCE: How do you know? What clues did you find in the text?

3. INFERENCE: How many miles did the Greek messenger run?

4. CONTEXT CLUES: What do you think *victory* means?

☐ win
☐ loss
☐ tie

5. S-T-R-E-T-C-H: Have you ever done a long and tiring activity? Describe it.

Remembering Jackie Robinson

On April 15, 1947, Jackie Robinson played his first game for the Brooklyn Dodgers. Not only was Robinson a great player, but he was also an important **figure** in history. He was the first African American to play Major League Baseball. His uniform number was 42. Robinson retired from baseball in 1956 and died in 1972. But his memory lives on. Each year on April 15, every Major League Baseball player wears a special uniform. They wear it no matter what team they're on: Yankees, Cubs, or Giants. The special uniform has a very special number on it, too—to honor the remarkable Jackie Robinson.

KEY QUESTIONS

1. INFERENCE: What number do all baseball players wear on their uniforms on April 15?

2. TEXT EVIDENCE: How do you know? What clues did you find in the text?

3. DETAILS: What year did Robinson retire from baseball?

4. CONTEXT CLUES: What do you think *figure* means?

☐ stripes
☐ team
☐ person

5. S-T-R-E-T-C-H: Jackie Robinson was a hero. Write about your own personal hero.

Star-Spangled Banner

Some **aspects** of the American flag have stayed the same. From the beginning of the founding of the United States, the flag has always had red and white stripes. It has always had stars in a field of blue. But some things have changed over time. The original flag had only 13 stars. By 1836, when Arkansas became a state, the number of stars had climbed to 25. In 1959, Hawaii joined the United States. Yet another new flag was created, this one featuring 50 stars. And that's been the American flag ever since.

KEY QUESTIONS

1. INFERENCE: What causes the American flag to change?

2. TEXT EVIDENCE: How do you know? What clues did you find in the text?

3. SEQUENCE OF EVENTS: Did Arkansas become a state after Hawaii?

4. CONTEXT CLUES: What do you think *aspects* means?

☐ sizes
☐ stripes
☐ parts or features

5. S-T-R-E-T-C-H: Would you like to see the American flag add another star? Tell why or why not.

45

The Buzz About Bees

Lots of people dislike bees. But bees are actually very helpful insects. They make honey, and they spread pollen from tree to tree, helping the trees produce fruit. Apples, pears, peaches, almonds, and cantaloupes are just some of the foods that bees help produce. Some people actually think being around bees is fun. Beekeepers are people who keep and take care of bees. They take special steps to avoid getting stung. They wear a **protective** suit and thick gloves. They also wear a net that covers their faces. This way, they can enjoy spending time with their bee buddies.

KEY QUESTIONS

1. INFERENCE: Do beekeepers get a lot of bee stings?

2. TEXT EVIDENCE: How do you know? What clues did you find in the text?

3. DETAILS: Name some foods that bees help produce.

4. CONTEXT CLUES: What do you think *protective* means?

☐ shiny
☐ safe
☐ large

5. S-T-R-E-T-C-H: Why do you think lots of people dislike bees? How could you change their minds?

46

Krakatoa!

In 1883, a volcano called Krakatoa erupted. Krakatoa was in what today is the country of Indonesia. For many years afterwards, sunsets were unusually red. Krakatoa was such a big volcano that it affected almost the entire world. There were red sunsets in places as far away as Africa and Europe. People in America also noticed these **vivid** red sunsets. In fact, some people in New Haven, Connecticut, even called the fire department, mistakenly thinking a big fire had broken out.

KEY QUESTIONS

1. INFERENCE: What caused the unusually red sunsets in New Haven, Connecticut?

2. TEXT EVIDENCE: How do you know? What clues did you find in the text?

3. SUMMARIZE: Summarize this passage in a few sentences.

4. CONTEXT CLUES: What do you think *vivid* means?

☐ pale
☐ powerful
☐ incorrect

5. S-T-R-E-T-C-H: Do you think someone made a video of Krakatoa erupting? Tell why or why not.

False Names

Pseudonym is a funny word. It means, "false name." The word is most often used to describe a writer's made-up name. Probably you have never heard of Daniel Handler. You may know him instead by his pseudonym, Lemony Snicket. How about Stanley Lieber? He used the pseudonym Stan Lee to create comic book characters such as Spider-Man and the Hulk. Then there's Theodor Seuss Geisel. He wrote a series of **classic** kids' books. But his real name didn't appear on a single one. Instead the books all said "by Dr. Seuss."

KEY QUESTIONS

1. INFERENCE: What is Theodor Seuss Geisel's pseudonym?

2. TEXT EVIDENCE: How do you know? What clues did you find in the text?

3. DETAILS: What is the real name of the author of the Lemony Snicket books?

4. CONTEXT CLUES: What do you think *classic* means?

☐ bad and forgotten
☐ outstanding and remembered
☐ cat and hat

5. S-T-R-E-T-C-H: Make up your own pseudonym and describe what kind of books you'd write.

Cartoon Creation

It takes a lot of people to create the cartoons you watch on TV. The first thing that happens is a group of writers sits down and writes a really good story. Next, actors perform all the characters' lines. They do this just as if they were acting in front of the camera. But here, only their voices are recorded. The next step is to create all the **images**. Today, this is done by computer, but for many years, artists drew thousands and thousands of images by hand. Finally, all the pieces are put together, and the cartoon is ready for you to watch on TV.

KEY QUESTIONS

1. INFERENCE: Does making a cartoon require teamwork?

2. TEXT EVIDENCE: How do you know? What clues did you find in the text?

3. SUMMARIZE: Retell in a few sentences the steps of making a cartoon.

4. CONTEXT CLUES: What do you think *images* means?

☐ pictures
☐ music
☐ TV shows

5. S-T-R-E-T-C-H: Think of something you know how to do. Tell all the steps it takes, from start to finish.

Eat Your Spinach!

You've probably been told more than once to eat lots of fruits and vegetables. And kids aren't the only ones. Adults get this advice all the time, too. But what's so special about fruits and vegetables? Why is eating them so important? It turns out that vegetables and fruits are packed with vitamins that are good for our bodies. Foods like chips and candy, on the other hand, usually aren't very **nutritious**. Fruits and vegetables give us energy and help keep us healthy, now and in the future. Plus, they fill us up, so we don't eat too much junk food.

KEY QUESTIONS

1. INFERENCE: What is more nutritious, an orange or potato chips?

2. TEXT EVIDENCE: How do you know? What clues did you find in the text?'

3. MAIN IDEA: What is the main idea in this passage?

4. CONTEXT CLUES: What do you think *nutritious* means?

☐ healthy
☐ delicious
☐ filling

5. S-T-R-E-T-C-H: How many healthy snacks can you think of? Make a list.

Gold!

In 1848, a man named James Marshall discovered gold in California. There was gold in rivers and streams, and gold in the dirt. Marshall tried to keep his discovery a secret, but word soon got out. More than 300,000 people came from all over the country to dig for gold in the hopes of getting rich. This period, which lasted for about seven years, is known as the California Gold Rush. A few lucky people did find gold and got very rich. But the **majority** of people were disappointed.

They spent all their money to get to California and their dreams didn't come true.

KEY QUESTIONS

1. INFERENCE: Did the Gold Rush make lots of people rich?

2. TEXT EVIDENCE: How do you know? What clues did you find in the text?

3. SEQUENCE OF EVENTS: What happened after gold was discovered in 1848?

4. CONTEXT CLUES: What do you think *majority* means?

☐ very rich
☐ larger number
☐ smaller number

5. S-T-R-E-T-C-H: Why do you think James Marshall wanted to keep his discovery a secret? Explain.

INFERENCE: LITERARY

That's Spicy!

Eric and his family went to dinner at the new Mexican restaurant in town. Eric ordered three tacos. The waiter asked him if he wanted his tacos hot, medium, or mild. "Hot!" Eric replied. His mother looked over at him with a raised eyebrow. "Are you sure about that? Everyone else ordered mild." But Eric said he was sure. When the food arrived, everyone started eating. After Eric's first bite, his mouth was **ablaze**. He broke out in a sweat and his eyes began to water. He drank his entire glass of water and then gulped down his mom's. "Can I have some of your tacos instead?" he asked his sister.

KEY QUESTIONS

1. INFERENCE: Did Eric enjoy his tacos?

2. TEXT EVIDENCE: How do you know? What clues did you find in the text?

3. PREDICTION: Do you think Eric will order his food "hot" next time?

4. CONTEXT CLUES: What do you think *ablaze* means?

☐ sweet
☐ full
☐ on fire

5. S-T-R-E-T-C-H: Why do you think Eric's mom asks Eric if he's sure about his order? What makes you think so?

INFERENCE: LITERARY

Harry's Haircut

Harry's hair had gotten long and **unruly**. It was time to get a haircut. When he went to the barbershop, however, someone new was working there. For about half an hour, the man clipped away. When he had finished, he handed a mirror to Harry. "What do you think?" asked the barber. When Harry looked at himself, his heart sank. "Umm . . . thanks," he said, biting his lip. While he was walking to the car with his mother, Harry was eager for her opinion. "What do you think?" he asked nervously. "Well, the good news is that your hair grows very quickly," said his mother.

KEY QUESTIONS

1. INFERENCE: How did Harry feel about his haircut?

2. TEXT EVIDENCE: How do you know? What clues did you find in the text?

3. INFERENCE: Did Harry's mom like his haircut? How do you know?

4. CONTEXT CLUES: What do you think *unruly* means?

☐ neat
☐ messy
☐ dark

5. S-T-R-E-T-C-H: Turn on your imagination and describe a super-silly, terrible-looking haircut.

Sania's Snowman

There was fresh snow on the ground in Montana, and Sania decided to build a snowman. Sid stood nearby, eating a bag filled with shiny blue hard candy. "Hey, can I borrow your baseball cap?" Sania asked Sid. She placed the cap on the snowman's head. "Hey, can I borrow your scarf?" Sania asked Sid. She wrapped the scarf around the snowman's neck. But the snowman still required one last touch. He needed eyes. Sania searched around, but she couldn't find anything **suitable**. Then she came up with the perfect solution. *Plunk, plunk!* "Now my snowman has a cap, a scarf, and two shiny blue eyes," said Sania. "He's perfect!"

KEY QUESTIONS

1. INFERENCE: What did Sania use for the snowman's eyes?

2. TEXT EVIDENCE: How do you know? What clues did you find in the text?

3. SETTING: Where is this story set? What is the season?

4. CONTEXT CLUES: What do you think *suitable* means?

☐ correct
☐ wrong
☐ wearable

5. S-T-R-E-T-C-H: Describe a snowman you would make using surprising objects. Don't be afraid to get silly!

The Blueberry Fan

My little sister loves blueberries. She doesn't just like them, she's crazy for them! If you offered her some blueberries or a warm chocolate chip cookie, she would choose the blueberries. I mean, she's just nuts for them! What's her favorite ice cream flavor? Blueberry. What kind of jam does she like on her toast? You guessed it: Blueberry! Last weekend I was visiting my friend who lives on a farm. Her family actually *grows* blueberries! I thought how **elated** my sister would be if I came home with a big basket of fresh-picked blueberries. So I picked a whole bunch.

KEY QUESTIONS

1. INFERENCE: Do you think the narrator likes her little sister?

2. TEXT EVIDENCE: How do you know? What clues did you find in the text?

3. TONE: What is the tone of this story?

4. CONTEXT CLUES: What do you think *elated* means?

☐ hungry
☐ silly
☐ happy

5. S-T-R-E-T-C-H: What do you think happens next in the story? Write it.

INFERENCE: LITERARY

Last-Leaf Lenny

Lenny the Leaf was still green. It was late autumn, and he was the last leaf left on his branch. All his leaf friends had turned yellow, orange, and red. Then they'd snapped off the branch and floated down, down, down. Finally, they landed in a giant pile beneath the tree. Jump, jump! Kids jumped into the pile and played with the leaves. To Lenny, it looked like so much fun. He wanted to join his friends. Then, over a few days' time, Lenny began to change. He turned a brilliant red **hue**. Suddenly, he heard a snap and he was floating through the air. "Wheeeeeeee," said Lenny. "It's finally my turn."

KEY QUESTIONS

1. INFERENCE: Where did Lenny the Leaf land?

2. TEXT EVIDENCE: How do you know? What clues did you find in the text?

3. THEME: Which theme better fits this story: "Good things come to those who wait" or "A friend in need is a friend indeed." Why?

4. CONTEXT CLUES: What do you think *hue* means?

- ☐ berry
- ☐ acorn
- ☐ color

5. S-T-R-E-T-C-H: Turn on your imagination and write a story about a character named Rhonda Raindrop.

INFERENCE: LITERARY

The Sandwich Sneak

Lucy left the kitchen table for just a moment. When she returned, her peanut butter and jelly sandwich was gone. Had her younger sister Amy eaten it? When Lucy asked, Amy shook her head. What about her younger brother Gary? He made a face and added that he didn't like peanut butter. *Grrrr!* Now, Lucy grew **livid**. Who ate her sandwich? Next, she asked her youngest brother, 2-year-old Stu. Stu simply shook his head. When Lucy looked closely, however, she noticed something strange about Stu. Above his top lip, he had what looked like a little brown and purple mustache.

KEY QUESTIONS

1. INFERENCE: Who ate Lucy's sandwich?

2. TEXT EVIDENCE: How do you know? What clues did you find in the text?

3. SETTING: Where does this story take place?

4. CONTEXT CLUES: What do you think *livid* means?

- ☐ very happy
- ☐ very silly
- ☐ very mad

5. S-T-R-E-T-C-H: Do you think Stu knew what he was doing was wrong? Why or why not?

An Ice Cream Day

It was a hot summer day. Noah came inside after playing basketball with his friends. "Mom," he yelled. "Can I have some ice cream?" His mother called back: "Okay, but just one scoop. Then we're going to visit Grandma." Noah dished up one scoop of Super-Fudgy-Ripple ice cream. He was just finishing his last spoonful, when his mom **declared** that it was time to go, and they jumped into the car. "It sure is hot," his mom said a few minutes later. "Did you remember to put the ice cream back in the freezer?" *Uh-oh*, thought Noah. Then his heart sank.

KEY QUESTIONS

1. INFERENCE: What happened to the ice cream?

2. TEXT EVIDENCE: How do you know? What clues did you find in the text?

3. DETAILS: What kind of ice cream did Noah eat?

4. CONTEXT CLUES: What do you think *declared* means?

☐ said
☐ forgot
☐ changed her mind

5. S-T-R-E-T-C-H: Have you ever forgotten to put something away? What happened?

Ping-Pong Problem

Best friends Jill and Jason were in the basement playing a game of ping-pong. It was match point. Jill served up the ball smoothly. Jason returned it. Back and forth, back and forth went the ball. Finally, the ball bounced off a corner of the table. Jason **lunged** for it. He dropped his paddle and threw up his arms. Then he stormed out of the basement frowning. When Jill went upstairs, her friend was playing a video game. "Let's play this," said Jason. "I bet I can beat you." Jill said, "Maybe later. Let's get a snack."

KEY QUESTIONS

1. INFERENCE: Who lost the game of ping-pong?

2. TEXT EVIDENCE: How do you know? What clues did you find in the text?

3. CHARACTER: How would you describe Jason?

4. CONTEXT CLUES: What do you think *lunged* means?

☐ ignored
☐ danced
☐ moved suddenly forward

5. S-T-R-E-T-C-H: Is it important to be a good loser? Write about it.

First Time Sledding

Gina had never seen snow before. That's not surprising, because she lived in Florida. Over holiday break, however, she visited her cousin Val in Colorado. On the first evening, big snowflakes began to fall. "If this keeps up, we'll be able to sled tomorrow for sure," said Val. That gave Gina a fluttery feeling in her stomach, like falling snow. She could barely sleep that night. The next morning, Gina jumped out of bed and **peered** through the window. Wow! The ground was covered in a thick blanket of fluffy, white snow. "Wake up, Val!" she shouted.

KEY QUESTIONS

1. INFERENCE: How does Gina feel when she sees the snow?

2. TEXT EVIDENCE: How do you know? What clues did you find in the text?

3. INFERENCE: Does it snow in Florida? How do you know?

4. CONTEXT CLUES: What do you think *peered* means?

☐ yelled
☐ listened
☐ looked

5. S-T-R-E-T-C-H: What's something you've never done but would like to try? Write about it.

Wanda Is Wild for Wolves

Yesterday, I visited my friend Wanda. She was wearing a T-shirt with a picture of a wolf on it. When her mother poured us juice, the cups had wolves on them. Then, we watched a movie about wolves. When it was time for bed, Wanda changed into her wolf pajamas. Then she slipped into her bed, which was covered in a blanket with a life-like **depiction** of a beautiful gray wolf howling at the full moon. Wanda's birthday is coming up. I was in the bookstore yesterday and I saw a book about wolves. So I bought it and wrapped it in paper covered in little pictures of . . . well, you guessed it!

KEY QUESTIONS

1. INFERENCE: What are the pictures on the wrapping paper for Wanda's present?

2. TEXT EVIDENCE: How do you know? What clues did you find in the text?

3. TONE: What is the tone of this story?

4. CONTEXT CLUES: What do you think *depiction* means?

☐ pillow
☐ sheet
☐ picture

5. S-T-R-E-T-C-H: What do you think Wanda's bedroom looks like? Describe it.

Candy Overload

Oliver was crazy for candy. Chocolate bars, jelly beans, licorice, toffee. He loved it all. His favorite holiday was Halloween. He loved dressing up in a costume and seeing all the spooky decorations. But what he loved most was coming home with a big bag **brimming** with CANDY. This year, as soon as he got home from trick-or-treating, his mom took his bag and said, "I'll keep an eye on this." Oliver frowned. "But it's my candy," he said. His mother hugged him. "But remember what happened last year?" Oliver thought back to last Halloween and his stomach began to hurt. "Oh, yeah," he said. "You'd better take it."

KEY QUESTIONS

1. INFERENCE: What happened last Halloween?

2. TEXT EVIDENCE: How do you know? What clues did you find in the text?

3. CHARACTER: How would you describe Oliver's mom?

4. CONTEXT CLUES: What do you think *brimming* means?

☐ filled
☐ empty
☐ melted

5. S-T-R-E-T-C-H: Eating lots and lots of candy is an example of "too much of a good thing." Can you think of some other examples?

Smooth Sailing?

Deena's grandfather lived by a big lake. He had his own sailboat, and for months, Deena had begged him to take her sailing. She'd never been on a boat before. Today was finally the day! As they hopped aboard, her grandfather said, "It looks like the water might be a little rough. That will make it fun!" He steered the boat over the choppy water, and Deena began feeling **queasy**. "Isn't this great?" her grandfather asked. "Uh, yeah," Deena replied. She held onto the sides of the boat so hard her knuckles turned white. Water sprayed into the boat, soaking her shorts. "Grandpa, when can we go home?" Deena asked.

KEY QUESTIONS

1. INFERENCE: Was Deena having a good time on the boat?

2. TEXT EVIDENCE: How do you know? What clues did you find in the text?

3. PREDICTION: Do you think Deena will go sailing again? Explain why.

4. CONTEXT CLUES: What do you think *queasy* means?

☐ nauseated
☐ intelligent
☐ cold

5. S-T-R-E-T-C-H: Have you ever looked forward to something, only to have it turn out differently than you expected? Tell about it.

Third Time's the Charm

In class, the kids were doing origami. Origami is a type of Japanese art where a piece of paper is folded into a shape. Juan wanted to make a swan, and he would not give up until he did so. On his first try, he folded the paper, then folded it some more. But it didn't end up looking like much of anything. So Juan tried again. This time the folded paper was a messy shape. If you turned it just so, maybe it looked slightly like a frog. It sure didn't **resemble** a swan. So Juan tried a third time, and his creation looked perfect. "Finally!" he exclaimed. "The third time's the charm."

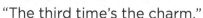

KEY QUESTIONS

1. INFERENCE: On his third try, what origami shape does Juan make?

2. TEXT EVIDENCE: How do you know? What clues did you find in the text?

3. INFERENCE: Why does Juan say, "The third time's the charm?"

4. CONTEXT CLUES: What do you think *resemble* means?

☐ put back together
☐ fold poorly
☐ look like

5. S-T-R-E-T-C-H: Describe a time you had to try several times to learn a new skill.

Bad Planning

Iris was 13 and her brother, Jake, was 10. She and Jake were going to the movies. They planned to walk because the movie theater was only three blocks away. Jake **cautioned** that it looked like it was going to rain. "Let's bring umbrellas," he said. Iris hated the rain, and she hated getting wet. But she looked up at the sky and thought the clouds looked friendly. "I don't think it's going to rain," she said. "Well, I'm bringing an umbrella," Jake said. On their way to the theater it started to pour. "Ack!" Iris screamed. She tried to fit under Jake's umbrella, but she got wet anyway. "I told you," Jake said.

KEY QUESTIONS

1. INFERENCE: Does Iris wish she'd brought an umbrella?

2. TEXT EVIDENCE: How do you know? What clues did you find in the text?

3. THEME: Which theme better fits this story: "Be careful what you wish for" or "It's good to be prepared"?

4. CONTEXT CLUES: What do you think *cautioned* means?

☐ warned
☐ hoped
☐ decided

5. S-T-R-E-T-C-H: Can you think of 10 or more words to describe rain? Make a list!

Marble Magic

Lately, Gina's little brother, Joel, was into magic tricks. He often tried them out on Gina. They never worked.

"Think of a number between one and ten," Joel said. "Now I'm going to reach into this old sock for a handful of marbles." Joel reached into the old sock. He held out his closed fist. "Now, I'll open my hand and we'll count the marbles." He opened his hand and there were seven marbles. "Is that the number you were thinking of?" he asked. Gina was **astonished** and let out a surprised laugh. "Wow! I guess I REALLY am magic!" shouted Joel.

KEY QUESTIONS

1. INFERENCE: What number was Gina thinking of?

2. TEXT EVIDENCE: How do you know? What clues did you find in the text?

3. CHARACTER: Think of three words to describe Joel.

4. CONTEXT CLUES: What do you think *astonished* means?

☐ bored
☐ hungry
☐ amazed

5. S-T-R-E-T-C-H: Do you think Joel will be able to do the trick again, or did he just get lucky this time? Tell why you think so.

The Birthday Dinner

Cabbage was Bart's favorite food. There was only one problem: He hated the way it smelled when his mother cooked it. So his mom came up with a great idea. "Whenever I cook cabbage, I'll also burn a scented candle," said his mom. "That will help **mask** the smell." A few days later, it was Bart's birthday. When he arrived home from school, a candle was burning. The air had a pleasant smell, like roses. "I'm really looking forward to my birthday dinner," said Bart with a grin.

KEY QUESTIONS

1. INFERENCE: Name a food Bart is getting with his birthday dinner.

2. TEXT EVIDENCE: How do you know? What clues did you find in the text?

3. INFERENCE: Is Bart's mother thoughtful? How do you know?

4. CONTEXT CLUES: What do you think *mask* means?

☐ forget
☐ increase
☐ hide

5. S-T-R-E-T-C-H: What is your favorite food? Describe it.

INFERENCE: LITERARY

Bad Table Manners

The dinner table was all set, waiting. When the family was nearby, the plates, forks, and other dinner items had to remain silent. These items knew how to talk, but they had to pretend otherwise. Right now, the family was on the other side of the house. So the table settings got into an argument. "You're not very sharp," said the glass to the knife. "I can see right through you," retorted the knife. "You seem shaky tonight," said the pepper to the salt. "You make me want to sneeze," **retorted** the salt. "Shhhhhh . . . everyone," said the butter dish. "I hear the family coming."

KEY QUESTIONS

1. INFERENCE: In this story, what special human ability would a spoon have?

2. TEXT EVIDENCE: How do you know? What clues did you find in the text?

3. TONE: What is the tone of this story?

4. CONTEXT CLUES: What do you think *retorted* means?

- ☐ slowly answered
- ☐ sharply answered
- ☐ sweetly answered

5. S-T-R-E-T-C-H: Create some more dialogue among these talkative table settings.

INFERENCE: LITERARY

B-Ball Turnaround

When it came to basketball, Amna felt like a failure. She never made baskets, and the coach hardly ever let her play. Her dad said lots of practice was the key to getting better. He put up a hoop in the yard, and Amna practiced shooting, dribbling, and doing layups. Slowly, she improved. But she still **seldom** got to play. Then late one game, Mia, the star player, twisted her ankle, and the coach put Amna in. The game was tied, and the coach looked worried. But Amna's hours of practice paid off. She scored the winning basket. She leapt into the air. Everyone yelled, "Am-na! Am-na!" She didn't stop smiling for days.

KEY QUESTIONS

1. INFERENCE: How does Amna feel at the end of the story?

2. TEXT EVIDENCE: How do you know? What clues did you find in the text?

3. CHARACTER: How would you describe Amna?

4. CONTEXT CLUES: What do you think *seldom* means?

- ☐ rarely
- ☐ always
- ☐ weekly

5. S-T-R-E-T-C-H: Why didn't the coach let Amna play very much? What would you do if you were Amna?

Sweet Relief

Jordan had just heard a catchy new song. Now, she sang it **incessantly**. While hanging out with her friend, Nia, every few seconds Jordan broke into the song. During lunch, Jordan took a bite of pizza, then she burst out singing. She took a sip of lemonade and then—the song. That afternoon, the girls went to the swimming pool. Nia got on the diving board. Right behind her was Jordan, waiting her turn, still singing that song. Nia dove into the pool. She stayed underwater as long as she could, holding her breath. Ah, sweet relief!

KEY QUESTIONS

1. INFERENCE: How does Nia feel about the song?

2. TEXT EVIDENCE: How do you know? What clues did you find in the text?

3. PREDICTION: What will happen when Nia comes back out of the water?

4. CONTEXT CLUES: What do you think *incessantly* means?

☐ constantly
☐ beautifully
☐ out of tune

5. S-T-R-E-T-C-H: "Sweet relief" is both the title and last line of this story. Why do you think the author made this choice?

The Pipers Pick Their Pumpkins

The Pipers were a family of five. For Halloween, they all picked their own pumpkins. Mr. Piper was the biggest, so he chose the biggest pumpkin. He carved it into a jack-o'-lantern with a goofy grin. Mrs. Piper picked the second biggest pumpkin. Her jack-o'-lantern had a round mouth and looked surprised. Penny and Pearl were the ten-year-old Piper twins. They picked the third-biggest pumpkins, which were exactly the same size. Penny's jack-o'-lantern had a giant smile, while Pearl's had the opposite—a **grimace**. Perry Piper was just three. His jack-o'-lantern had four eyes, one nose, and two mouths. Why? Because that was what Perry wanted.

KEY QUESTIONS

1. INFERENCE: Which family member got the smallest pumpkin?

2. TEXT EVIDENCE: How do you know? What clues did you find in the text?

3. INFERENCE: In what season does this story take place? How do you know?

4. CONTEXT CLUES: What do you think *grimace* means?

☐ mouth
☐ smile
☐ scowl

5. S-T-R-E-T-C-H: Describe the jack-o'-lantern face you would carve.

Lost and Found

Milo couldn't find his calculator anywhere. He searched all over the classroom. "Why don't you check the lost and found?" said Ms. Kim. So Milo went to the main office. The school secretary brought out a big box. When Milo looked inside, sure enough, there was his calculator. As he reached for it, he also noticed his missing sweater. Underneath the sweater was his missing hat, headphones, and wallet. The wallet still contained the $3 he'd lost. Milo thanked the secretary. Then, he **departed** the office with an armload of found items.

KEY QUESTIONS

1. INFERENCE: Is Milo good at keeping track of his possessions?

2. TEXT EVIDENCE: How do you know? What clues did you find in the text?

3. PREDICTION: What do you think will happen to the items Milo got from the lost and found?

4. CONTEXT CLUES: What do you think *departed* means?

☐ arrived
☐ stayed
☐ left

5. S-T-R-E-T-C-H: What are some items that you have lost? List what your own personal "lost and found" box would contain.

The Favorite

Being the family's favorite pet is a pretty sweet deal. I have all my meals prepared for me every day. Whenever I hear my humans pop open the can of food, I stop chasing the silly dog and come running! Another great benefit is that I get lots of soft pats on my head, down my back, and under my chin. Sometimes I **vault** onto someone's lap and curl up in a ball. Then I purr really loudly, and they stroke my head and tell me how good I am. The dog thinks he's the favorite, but I know I'm the one they really love.

FLUFFY

KEY QUESTIONS

1. INFERENCE: What kind of animal is the narrator?

2. TEXT EVIDENCE: How do you know? What clues did you find in the text?

3. TONE: What is the tone of the story?

4. CONTEXT CLUES: What do you think *vault* means?

☐ pet
☐ curl
☐ jump

5. S-T-R-E-T-C-H: Imagine this story is told from the dog's point of view. Write it!

Freckle Face

"I wish I could wash away my freckles!" Katy said to her mom when she got home from school. "A bunch of kids teased me today, calling me Freckle Face. They said freckles are weird." Her mom looked at her in surprise. "Do you think I look weird?" her mom **inquired**. "No," Katy said. "I think you look beautiful." "But I have lots of freckles," her mom said. "My face is covered in them." Katy looked at her mom's face. It was true. She did have lots of freckles. And she loved her mom's face. "Hmmm," said Katy "You've made me change my mind about freckles . . . again."

KEY QUESTIONS

1. INFERENCE: How does Katy feel about freckles at the START of the story?

2. TEXT EVIDENCE: How do you know? What clues did you find in the text?

3. INFERENCE: Does Katy like freckles at the END of the story? How do you know?

4. CONTEXT CLUES: What do you think *inquired* means?

☐ cried
☐ washed
☐ asked

5. S-T-R-E-T-C-H: What happens next in the story? Write it

A Snowy Walk

Sean and his mom and their big dog, Penny, were out for a walk in the woods. There had been a major snowfall that morning. But now the sun was out and the ground was covered with fresh white snow. As they walked, Penny stayed by their side. But when they reached their neighbor's barn, she took off and **sprinted** ahead. Sean and his mom came to a spot where the path split in two directions. Both directions led back home. The path on the right had smooth, unbroken snow. On the left, Sean noticed paw prints in the snow. "Let's take the path Penny took," Sean said.

KEY QUESTIONS

1. INFERENCE: Which path did Sean and his mom take?

2. TEXT EVIDENCE: How do you know? What clues did you find in the text?

3. SETTING: What season is it in the story?

4. CONTEXT CLUES: What do you think *sprinted* means?

☐ barked
☐ ran
☐ turned around

5. S-T-R-E-T-C-H: Does Sean live in the city or the country? How do you know?

INFERENCE: LITERARY

Rapunzel's New Hairdo

Rapunzel lived at the top of a tall tower. She had **exceedingly** long hair. Each day, the Prince stood outside and called: "Rapunzel, let down your golden hair." Up he climbed. They'd hang out in her room reading and playing video games. One day, Rapunzel decided to give herself a new hairdo. Snip, snip. When the Prince arrived, he called, "Rapunzel, let down your golden hair." But now her hair was bright pink. What's more, it hung only a tiny way down the tower wall. "I guess I'll have to go up the normal way," said the Prince. Then he set out climbing the tower stairs.

KEY QUESTIONS

1. INFERENCE: After Rapunzel gets a new hairdo, why can't the Prince climb her hair?

2. TEXT EVIDENCE: How do you know? What clues did you find in the text?

3. TONE: Is the Prince deeply in love with Rapunzel? How do you know?

4. CONTEXT CLUES: What do you think *exceedingly* means?

☐ very
☐ blonde
☐ messy

5. S-T-R-E-T-C-H: Make up a fairy tale about Rapunzel and her pink hair.

INFERENCE: LITERARY

Untitled Tale

Thelma Thumb learned where food could be found, but getting there would require an **epic** journey. She climbed on a leaf and sailed across a puddle. She found a piece of string and tied it around a flower stem. Then she stepped out of her leaf-boat and climbed to the top of an anthill. Next, she hiked through the tall blades of grass. At last, she arrived at the sidewalk. There it was! To Thelma, the empty potato chip bag looked like a cave. Deep inside, she found a few crumbs. Thelma lifted the heavy crumbs and put them in her backpack. Now she had enough food to last a week. Mission accomplished.

KEY QUESTIONS

1. INFERENCE: What size is Thelma Thumb?

2. TEXT EVIDENCE: How do you know? What clues did you find in the text?

3. INFERENCE: What size do you think Thelma's home is? What might it be made of?

4. CONTEXT CLUES: What do you think *epic* means?

☐ tiny and brave
☐ big and heroic
☐ sad and lonely

5. S-T-R-E-T-C-H: This story is called "Untitled Tale." Now that you've read it, what would you call it?

Postponed

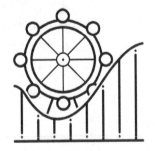

Jamal woke up early because they were going to the amusement park that day. "What time . . . *achoo!* . . . are we going?" he asked his dad. "I can't wait to ride the . . . *achoo!* . . . Big Dipper." Jamal reached for a tissue and blew his nose. "Are you feeling okay?" his dad asked. Jamal sneezed a few more times and let out a **thunderous** cough. "I'm feeling . . . *achoo!* . . . great," he said. His dad rested his hand on Jamal's forehead. "Uh-oh. I think we might have to make our trip to the amusement park next weekend," he said.

KEY QUESTIONS

1. INFERENCE: Why does Jamal's dad say they will have to go next weekend?

2. TEXT EVIDENCE: How do you know? What clues did you find in the text?

3. SETTING: What time of day does this story take place?

4. CONTEXT CLUES: What do you think *thunderous* means?

☐ very funny
☐ very quiet
☐ very loud

5. S-T-R-E-T-C-H: Why is the story called "Postponed"?

The Right Horse

Brie went to the stables to go horseback riding. "Pancake is a gentle horse, perfect for a beginner," said the man who cared for the horses. "Pepper is a bit **ornery**. She can be cranky and does what she wants." But Brie thought Pepper was a beautiful horse. "I choose Pepper," Brie told the stable owner. When they got out on the trail, Pepper tried to break into a run. "Whoa, girl," said Brie. Brie was firm with the reins and talked to Pepper in a calm, confident voice. Soon, Pepper began to behave, and followed Brie's every command. She'd picked the right horse.

KEY QUESTIONS

1. INFERENCE: What kind of rider is Brie?

2. TEXT EVIDENCE: How do you know? What clues did you find in the text?

3. PREDICTION: What would happen if an inexperienced rider chose Pepper?

4. CONTEXT CLUES: What do you think *ornery* means?

☐ four-legged
☐ bad-tempered
☐ fast-running

5. S-T-R-E-T-C-H: Which horse would you choose, Pancake or Pepper? Write about it.

INFERENCE: LITERARY

The Legend of Rooster

This is a legend about why roosters say "cock-a-doodle-doo." Rooster lived happily with his friends. Then, one day, many exciting things happened. Dog fell into the pond. Horse almost ran away. Snake crawled into the barn. That night, Rooster wanted to tell his friend Cow about the day's events. "Shush," said Cow sleepily, "save it for the sunrise." But Rooster was so excited. It took him awhile to fall asleep. When he awoke—yippee!—it was finally time to tell Cow everything that had happened. By now, though, Rooster had waited so long and had grown so excited that his words **jumbled** together. So he simply shouted, "cock-a-doodle-doo!"

KEY QUESTIONS

1. INFERENCE: What time of day did Rooster say, "cock-a-doodle-doo?"

2. TEXT EVIDENCE: How do you know? What clues did you find in the text?

3. SETTING: Where does this story take place?

4. CONTEXT CLUES: What do you think *jumbled* means?

☐ yelled
☐ chattered
☐ mixed up

5. S-T-R-E-T-C-H: Make up a reason why an animal makes its sound and write about it.

INFERENCE: LITERARY

Weird World of Sports

Gabby Goonsby here, reporting for Weird World of Sports. I have incredible news! This year's tennis champion is Baxter Beaver. Let's watch the video. Look at him play, folks! Just take a look at his **formidable** tail. It's wide and powerful. When Baxter swings his tail, the other tennis players don't stand a chance. Baxter may only be two feet, six inches tall, but he's a tennis superstar! After the break, I'll be back with news about the sensational Sandy Shark's upcoming swim race. In fact, I'll have an exclusive interview with this undefeated champ.

KEY QUESTIONS

1. INFERENCE: What body part does Baxter Beaver use to hit the tennis ball?

2. TEXT EVIDENCE: How do you know? What clues did you find in the text?

3. PREDICTION: Do you think Sandy Shark will win her next swim race? Why or why not?

4. CONTEXT CLUES: What do you think *formidable* means?

☐ feathery
☐ shapeless
☐ impressive

5. S-T-R-E-T-C-H: Pretend you're the sportscaster at Sandy Shark's swim race. Write a mini-story about it.

INFERENCE: LITERARY

Good Things Come in Small and Large Packages

Twelve-year-old Mia and her mother were exchanging holiday gifts. Mia opened hers first. It came in a **mammoth** package. She tore off the wrapping paper. She ripped open the box. It was a bicycle! "This is exactly what I wanted," said Mia. Now, it was her mother's turn to get a gift. "I saved my allowance for a whole month to buy this for you," said Mia. The present came in a little package. Mia's mother peeled off the wrapping paper. She opened the tiny box. "This is exactly what I wanted," she said. She put the gift on her finger. How it sparkled!

KEY QUESTIONS

1. INFERENCE: What gift did Mia's mother receive?

2. TEXT EVIDENCE: How do you know? What clues did you find in the text?

3. INFERENCE: Do you think the gift Mia got for her mother cost $20 or $20,000? Why?

4. CONTEXT CLUES: What do you think *mammoth* means?

☐ very small
☐ very large
☐ extinct

5. S-T-R-E-T-C-H: Write about something great that might come in a tiny package.

INFERENCE: LITERARY

The Baby Birds

One morning, Aki heard birds chirping outside his window. He looked out and saw a nest in the big oak tree. Inside were three **fledglings**. They tried to flap their wings, but they were still too small. Just then, their mother swooped into the nest. She fed them from her beak. *Wow*, Aki thought. *It's like a nature show right outside my window!* In the days that followed, Aki heard the baby birds as soon as he woke up. He watched them practice flapping their wings. Every day they were a little bit bigger. Then one morning he awoke and heard . . . nothing. He ran to the window. The birds were gone!

KEY QUESTIONS

1. INFERENCE: What happened to the birds?

2. TEXT EVIDENCE: How do you know? What clues did you find in the text?

3. CHARACTER: What kind of person do you think Aki is?

4. CONTEXT CLUES: What do you think *fledglings* means?

☐ baby birds
☐ oak trees
☐ wings

5. S-T-R-E-T-C-H: What is your favorite type of bird? Why?

The Present

Micah's grandmother told him that a special present would be arriving for him on Tuesday. That afternoon, Micah sat on the porch. He **glanced** up and down the block, searching for the mail carrier, who would bring his package. She finally arrived and handed Micah the mail. But there was no package. "Are you sure that's all?" he asked. "Yep," she said, and went to the next house. Micah's disappointment was huge. But just then a truck pulled up. It said "Dave's Scooter Shop" on the side. The driver pulled a big box out of the truck and walked up to Micah and said, "I think this is for you." "Wow!" Micah said.

KEY QUESTIONS

1. INFERENCE: Why does Micah sit on the front porch?

2. TEXT EVIDENCE: How do you know? What clues did you find in the text?

3. PREDICTION: What do you think is in the box? Why?

4. CONTEXT CLUES: What do you think *glanced* means?

☐ ran
☐ looked
☐ shouted

5. S-T-R-E-T-C-H: Micah experiences different emotions in the story. What are they?

Opposite Man

Meet Opposite Man, world's worst superhero. Whatever is true of a regular superhero is not true of him. Most superheroes are strong. Opposite Man is super weak. In one of his adventures, he is struck by a falling leaf and knocked to the ground. Many superheroes can fly. Opposite Man has claws similar to a badger. Instead of flying, he burrows deep into the ground. All superheroes fight against bad guys. Well, all of them except for Opposite Man. He actually helps out evil **villains**. Would you like to NOT see a movie about Opposite Man?

KEY QUESTIONS

1. INFERENCE: Is Opposite Man brave?

2. TEXT EVIDENCE: How do you know? What clues did you find in the text?

3. PREDICTION: Would Opposite Man help a bank robber? Why do you think so?

4. CONTEXT CLUES: What do you think *villains* means?

☐ villagers
☐ good guys
☐ bad guys

5. S-T-R-E-T-C-H: Dream up a silly superhero and write about him or her.

A Baking Flop

Jewel loved to watch cooking shows on TV. When she grew up, she wanted to be a baker. *I'd better start practicing now*, she thought. She found a recipe called **Basic** Bread. All you needed was flour, water, and a little yeast. The recipe said the yeast would make the bread rise in the oven. But Jewel didn't have any yeast. The recipe called for just one teaspoon. *Just one tiny teaspoon?!* Jewel was sure the bread would be fine without it. She mixed everything and put it in the oven. But in the end the bread was as flat as a pancake.

KEY QUESTIONS

1. INFERENCE: What does yeast do for bread?

2. TEXT EVIDENCE: How do you know? What clues did you find in the text?

3. SETTING: In what room does this story take place?

4. CONTEXT CLUES: What do you think *basic* means?

- [ ] difficult
- [ ] simple
- [ ] hungry

5. S-T-R-E-T-C-H: Should you always follow a recipe exactly? Tell why or why not.

Messy Mo

Yasmin's dog, Mo, loved to get dirty. He rolled in the grass and **scampered** through the mud. If there was a puddle, Mo splashed in it. That afternoon, after a morning of rain, Yasmin's mom asked her to take Mo outside. "Make sure he doesn't get dirty," her mom said. Mo tore off and ran through the wet and muddy yard. Yasmin grabbed a towel to wipe Mo's dirty paws. But before she could catch him, Mo ran into the house and jumped on the clean white sofa. "Uh-oh," Yasmin said.

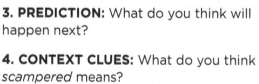

KEY QUESTIONS

1. INFERENCE: Why does Yasmin say "Uh-oh" at the end of the story?

2. TEXT EVIDENCE: How do you know? What clues did you find in the text?

3. PREDICTION: What do you think will happen next?

4. CONTEXT CLUES: What do you think *scampered* means?

- [ ] ran
- [ ] barked
- [ ] tiptoed

5. S-T-R-E-T-C-H: Write the next scene of this story.

Blooming Daffodils

In September, Lorenzo helped his mom plant daffodils in their yard. Over the next several weeks, Lorenzo went out to the yard and looked to see if the flowers were sprouting. But all he **detected** was dirt. His mother explained that the flowers were growing very slowly underneath the soil. They would stay beneath the earth all winter. Then, when spring came and the weather turned warmer, the daffodils would push through the soil and bloom. As the months went by, Lorenzo forgot all about the daffodils. But then one Saturday, he spotted a patch of bright yellow in the backyard.

KEY QUESTIONS

1. INFERENCE: What does Lorenzo see at the end of the story?

2. TEXT EVIDENCE: How do you know? What clues did you find in the text?

3. INFERENCE: What season is it at the end of the story? How do you know?

4. CONTEXT CLUES: What do you think *detected* means?

- ☐ planted
- ☐ noticed
- ☐ forgot

5. S-T-R-E-T-C-H: Have you ever planted seeds or gardened? Would you like to? Write about it.

I Don't Want to Go to Sleep!

Ruby was a bear cub, and this was her first winter. She knew she was supposed to sleep during the coldest months, but she didn't want to **hibernate**. She wanted to climb trees and play with the other cubs! Her mother explained that winters were freezing and there wasn't any food to eat. They had to save their energy until spring. But Ruby thought that sounded very boring. So she made a plan. When everyone else was asleep, she would sneak out of their den and go have fun. But then, suddenly, she felt very, very tired. So she curled up beside her mom and slept. Zzzzz.

KEY QUESTIONS

1. INFERENCE: Who knows better, Ruby or her mother?

2. TEXT EVIDENCE: How do you know? What clues did you find in the text?

3. CHARACTER: How would you describe Ruby's character?

4. CONTEXT CLUES: What do you think *hibernate* means?

- ☐ sleep during winter
- ☐ eat during winter
- ☐ dance during winter

5. S-T-R-E-T-C-H: What do you think Ruby did when she woke up in the spring? Turn on your imagination and tell about it!

A Perfect Birthday

Miguel spent his twelfth birthday with his good friend Lucas, doing the thing he loved best. His mom picked up Lucas and drove the boys to their destination. "I'll see you in two hours," she said. "Enjoy the show!" Miguel bought two tickets and gave one to Lucas. They handed the tickets to a man in a black vest. Then they stood in line and bought big bags of popcorn

with extra butter. They found two seats about 10 rows from the front. Just as they sat down, the lights **dimmed** and the screen came to life. Miguel was as happy as could be!

KEY QUESTIONS

1. INFERENCE: Where are Miguel and Lucas?

2. TEXT EVIDENCE: How do you know? What clues did you find in the text?

3. PREDICTION: What do you think happens next in the story?

4. CONTEXT CLUES: What do you think *dimmed* means?

☐ got louder
☐ got darker
☐ got clearer

5. S-T-R-E-T-C-H: What would your perfect birthday be like? Write about it.

Sleepyhead

It was time to go to sleep, but Amelia couldn't stop reading her book. She had to find out what happened next. She looked at the clock, and told herself: *I know it's late. Just a few more pages.* She kept on reading and reading and reading. Finally, her eyelids began to droop, and she fell asleep. In the morning, when her alarm went off, she kept sleeping. Her dad came in and said: "Amelia! Time to get up!" But she kept on **slumbering**. Then her brother came in, stood next to her bed, and started playing his trumpet. And THAT got Amelia out of bed.

KEY QUESTIONS

1. INFERENCE: Why is Amelia so tired in the morning?

2. TEXT EVIDENCE: How do you know? What clues did you find in the text?

3. INFERENCE: Why do you think the trumpet gets Amelia out of bed?

4. CONTEXT CLUES: What do you think *slumbering* means?

☐ reading
☐ sleeping
☐ forgetting

5. S-T-R-E-T-C-H: Have you ever had a hard time getting out of bed? What happened?

The Recital

Jackie and her friend Felipe both took violin lessons. They were going to play in the recital next week. "I'm nervous," Jackie told Felipe. "The piece I'm going to play is really hard. I need to practice a LOT." Felipe said his piece was **challenging** too, but he wasn't worried. "I'll practice it a little, if I have the time. It'll go great." Jackie frowned. "You'd better practice more than that!" she warned. "Lots of people are going to be there." On the day of the recital, Felipe made lots of mistakes when he played. His face burned with embarrassment. How he wished he'd listened to Jackie.

KEY QUESTIONS

1. INFERENCE: Does Felipe's recital go as he planned?

2. TEXT EVIDENCE: How do you know? What clues did you find in the text?

3. PREDICTION: What do you think Felipe will do the next time he has a recital?

4. CONTEXT CLUES: What do you think *challenging* means?

☐ easy
☐ hard
☐ short

5. S-T-R-E-T-C-H: What lesson did you learn from reading this story?

How Will I Do It?

Clarence the caterpillar was worried. He was afraid he wouldn't know how to become a butterfly. His caterpillar pals told him to stop worrying. "It'll be easy. First you'll eat some leaves. You'll hang from a twig for a few weeks. You'll shed your skin and form a chrysalis. And then, *poof!* Butterfly!" Still, Clarence worried he wouldn't know how to do it. He got so nervous that he stuffed himself with leaves. He **anxiously** hung from a twig and worried for weeks. He still

worried as he shed his skin and formed a chrysalis. But then one day he felt something strange on his back. He had grown two beautiful wings!

KEY QUESTIONS

1. INFERENCE: Does Clarence become a butterfly?

2. TEXT EVIDENCE: How do you know? What clues did you find in the text?

3. CHARACTER: How would you describe Clarence?

4. CONTEXT CLUES: What do you think *anxiously* means?

☐ nervously
☐ happily
☐ quietly

5. S-T-R-E-T-C-H: Can you think of something else that changes from one thing to another? Write about it.

Raccoon Tan

Mila had a great visit to the ocean. The best part was her brand-new goggles. They kept the salty water from burning her eyes. Plus, she was amazed by what she could see underwater. Wearing the goggles **transformed** the experience of swimming in the water. It was thrilling to see all the little fish and crabs! Mila liked her goggles so much she even wore them to sit on the beach. When she got home, she noticed that her skin had tanned. Well—all except for around her eyes, where there were white circles. "Wow!" said Mila. "Somehow I got a raccoon tan."

KEY QUESTIONS

1. INFERENCE: What caused Mila to get a "raccoon tan"?

2. TEXT EVIDENCE: How do you know? What clues did you find in the text?

3. SETTING: Where does this story take place?

4. CONTEXT CLUES: What do you think *transformed* means?

- ☐ ruined
- ☐ traveled
- ☐ totally changed

5. S-T-R-E-T-C-H: Have you ever been to the ocean? Would you like to go? Write about it.

A Bad School Day

Jasmine and Kristi were best friends at school. But then Jasmine got the flu and had to stay in bed for two whole weeks. When she went back to school, she noticed that Kristi and another classmate, Elena, were now **inseparable**. They did everything together. When the teacher asked the class to pick a partner to do math problems, Kristi chose Elena. And that day at lunchtime, Kristi and Elena sat together eating their sandwiches. Kristi seemed to have forgotten all about Jasmine. When Jasmine got home from school, her mom asked, "How was your day?" Jasmine didn't respond—she just frowned.

KEY QUESTIONS

1. INFERENCE: Did Jasmine have a good day when she returned to school?

2. TEXT EVIDENCE: How do you know? What clues did you find in the text?

3. INFERENCE: How do you think Jasmine feels in the story?

4. CONTEXT CLUES: What do you think *inseparable* means?

- ☐ never together
- ☐ always together
- ☐ afraid

5. S-T-R-E-T-C-H: What could Jasmine do the next day at school so she doesn't feel left out?

Is It Broken?

Anika was playing soccer when she tripped over the ball and went tumbling. "Youch!" she screamed.

She ran over to her mom, trying not to cry. "My arm really hurts," she said. Her mom touched the arm **gingerly**, careful not to press too hard. "Is it broken?" Anika asked. "I think we better go to the emergency room," her mom said. The doctor at the hospital ordered an X-ray so he could see if the bone was broken. Then Anika and her mom waited. When the doctor came back, he said, "Good news! Just rest the arm for a few days and it will be just fine."

KEY QUESTIONS

1. INFERENCE: Is Anika's arm broken?

2. TEXT EVIDENCE: How do you know? What clues did you find in the text?

3. SETTING: The story starts off in the park. Where does it end?

4. CONTEXT CLUES: What do you think *gingerly* means?

☐ roughly
☐ carefully
☐ painfully

5. S-T-R-E-T-C-H: What are some other things that should be touched and handled gingerly? Make a list.

Time-Traveling Tomás

Tomás climbed inside the time machine. *Whoosh!* A few seconds passed, then he stepped outside. Dinosaurs were everywhere. A big, fierce-looking one came charging at him. Tomás jumped back inside the time machine. *Whoosh!* A few seconds passed, then he climbed out. Now, robots were everywhere. A **menacing** one rolled toward him, blinking its lights and saying, "Beep, bip, beep." Tomás hurried back into the time machine once more. *Whoosh!* A few seconds later, he got out. Everywhere there were cars, buildings, and people texting on cell phones. "I think I'll just stay here," thought Tomás.

KEY QUESTIONS

1. INFERENCE: In the end, what time period did Tomás decide to stay in?

2. TEXT EVIDENCE: How do you know? What clues did you find in the text?

3. INFERENCE: Did Tomás ever travel back in time? What clues did you find in the text?

4. CONTEXT CLUES: What do you think *menacing* means?

☐ funny
☐ fast
☐ threatening

5. S-T-R-E-T-C-H: Imagine Tomás gets into the time machine again. Write about where he goes next.

97

Wendy's Walls

The walls of Wendy's room were white. She asked her parents if she could paint them a new color. "How about blue?" she said. "That sounds great," her mom replied. But a few days later, Wendy changed her mind. "Bright yellow would be really cheerful." Then, after thinking a bit more, she decided on a light pink. "That sounds nice," her dad agreed. "Or maybe a lavender," Wendy said. "Or possibly lime green, or peach." There

were so many colors to choose from, how could she pick just one? Wendy was soooooooo **indecisive**. "Let's just keep the walls white," she said with a sigh.

KEY QUESTIONS

1. INFERENCE: Why does Wendy decide to leave the walls white?

2. TEXT EVIDENCE: How do you know? What clues did you find in the text?

3. CHARACTER: How would you describe Wendy?

4. CONTEXT CLUES: What do you think *indecisive* means?

☐ unable to see color
☐ unable to decide
☐ unable to laugh

5. S-T-R-E-T-C-H: What is your favorite color? Write about it.

98

Eye Trouble

Lately, Hector had trouble seeing things clearly. When his teacher wrote on the whiteboard, sometimes Hector had to **squint** to make it out.

When he watched a movie, the people's faces up on the screen often looked blurry. Now, Hector was at the mall with his mother. It was hard for Hector to read the store signs without walking up close to them. "Here we are. This is the store we want," said his mother. "Good," said Hector. "When I come back out, I hope I'll be able to see everything more clearly."

KEY QUESTIONS

1. INFERENCE: What kind of store does Hector go into?

2. TEXT EVIDENCE: How do you know? What clues did you find in the text?

3. SETTING: Where does this story take place?

4. CONTEXT CLUES: What do you think *squint* means?

☐ make a funny face
☐ spray water from a bottle
☐ close eyes partway

5. S-T-R-E-T-C-H: Glasses stores often have funny names like "See Here" or "Eye Love Glasses." Can you think of more? Make a list.

INFERENCE: LITERARY

Jaycee at the Bat

Jaycee was up next to bat. It was the bottom of the seventh inning. Her softball team was losing, 10 to 9. There was a runner on first base. If Jaycee could hit a home run, her team would win. Jaycee stepped up to home plate. The pitcher tossed the ball. Jaycee swung her bat hard. *Crack!* Jaycee took off running and just

kept going . . . until she reached home plate. Soon, everyone on her team was jumping up and down. Jaycee's coach was so proud. Even Jaycee's grumpy little brother, sitting in the stands, let out a **hearty** cheer.

KEY QUESTIONS

1. INFERENCE: What happened when Jaycee had her turn at bat?

2. TEXT EVIDENCE: How do you know? What clues did you find in the text?

3. PREDICTION: Do you think the other team was happy or sad? Why?

4. CONTEXT CLUES: What do you think *hearty* means?

☐ loud and annoying
☐ strong and loud
☐ weak and quiet

5. S-T-R-E-T-C-H: Do you have a favorite sport? Write about something exciting that happened when you were playing or watching it.

INFERENCE: LITERARY

A Trip to the Doctor

My little brother is such a scaredy-cat. When my mom told him he had to get a shot at the doctor's, you should have seen his face! He looked like he was going to run out of the building screaming. I told him to stop being such a chicken. "I've had shots before," I told him. "It's no big deal." While he saw the doctor, I waited in the waiting room. Then my mom came out and said, "Now it's your turn, Adam." My heart started beating fast and my knees began to **tremble**. "You m-m-mean I have to get a shot, too?" I stammered.

KEY QUESTIONS

1. INFERENCE: How does Adam feel about getting a shot?

2. TEXT EVIDENCE: How do you know? What clues did you find in the text?

3. CHARACTER: How would you describe Adam?

4. CONTEXT CLUES: What do you think *tremble* means?

☐ shake
☐ pretend
☐ look

5. S-T-R-E-T-C-H: Can you think of some other ways to show that a character is scared? Make a list.

INFERENCE: INFORMATIONAL

A Sport Is Born (Card 1)

1. James Naismith invented basketball.
2. The game is played inside. It's played during winter. The first games used peach baskets. Basketball is one of the most popular sports in the world.
3. In 1891, a gym teacher named James Naismith invented basketball so people could play an indoor winter sport. He used peach baskets and a ball. Everyone loved the game!
4. *Evolved* means "changed and grew."
5. Answers will vary.

The Missing *Mona Lisa* (Card 2)

1. No, the *Mona Lisa* was not world-famous in the 1600s.
2. The *Mona Lisa* didn't get international attention until someone had a sneaky plan in 1911.
3. Possible answers: It's a picture of a dark-haired woman with a sly smile. It was painted in 1506 by Leonardo da Vinci. It hangs in a museum in France.
4. *Outraged* means "angry."
5. Answers will vary.

Bugs, Bugs, Bugs! (Card 3)

1. There are more insects.
2. It says all the insects on the planet weigh MORE than all the people, so there must be a lot more insects than people.
3. There are a lot more insects on Earth than people.
4. *Measly* means "very small."
5. Answers will vary.

I'll Have a Scoop (Card 4)

1. No, it's available in other countries, too.
2. In Italy, they call it gelato.
3. Ice cream is called different things. It was a favorite treat of two presidents. It has been around a long time, but no one knows when it was invented. It is delicious!
4. *Historians* means "people who study the past."
5. Answers will vary.

What's in a (Street) Name? (Card 5)

1. It's very likely that the town would have a Main Street.
2. Main Street is the seventh most popular U.S. street name. America has 7,644 Main Streets.
3. This is the order of popularity: First Street, Main Street, Hill Street.
4. *Ubiquitous* means "widely used."
5. Answers will vary.

Bright Inventions (Card 6)

1. He invented the light bulb/the electric light.
2. Thomas Edison's invention used electricity to generate light.
3. The proper order is fire light, candle light, gas light, electric light.
4. *Generate* means "make."
5. Answers will vary.

Saving the Manatee (Card 7)

1. No, the number of manatees is no longer decreasing.
2. The outcome: This remarkable mammal was taken off the endangered species list.
3. Manatees are a large ocean mammal. Manatees were endangered because boats hurt them, but the government took action, so now the number of manatees is increasing.
4. *Habitats* means "homes."
5. Answers will vary.

Distance From the Sun (Card 8)

1. Neptune is cold.
2. Neptune is far from the sun, and the farther planets are from the sun, the colder they are.
3. Planets are warmer when they're closer to the sun and colder when they're far away.
4. *Dwell* means "live."
5. Jupiter is colder because it's farther from the sun.

Ye Olde Measurements (Card 9)

1. I would describe it as heavy.
2. If you tried to pick up a 10-stone barbell, you'd strain and sweat. It wouldn't budge.
3. I think its name is based on a candle.
4. *Strain* means "make great effort."
5. The puppy weighs 14 pounds. The boy weighs 56 pounds. The refrigerator weighs 280 pounds.

About Albert Einstein (Card 10)

1. Yes, he was an important scientist.
2. Some of his ideas changed how people understand the cosmos. And he won the Nobel Prize.
3. Einstein was a very important scientist.
4. *Cosmos* means "universe."
5. Answers will vary.

Chimps Like Us (Card 11)

1. Yes, they're similar.
2. They use tools like humans. They communicate, sometimes disagree, and have leaders. They kiss and hug and pat each other on the back.
3. Answers will vary.
4. *Relocated* means "moved."
5. Answers will vary.

A Spoonful a Day (Card 12)

1. Cod liver oil tastes terrible.
2. When kids were offered cod liver oil they shook their heads, scrunched up their faces, and shut their mouths super-tight.
3. Possible answer: Cod liver oil is something kids took in the old days. It was good for you, but tasted terrible.
4. *Ingredients* means "parts that make up it."
5. Answers will vary.

Surprising Snakes (Card 13)

1. A snake's skin would feel dry.
2. Even though it's shiny, it doesn't feel damp. It feels the opposite.
3. Possible answer: Snakes are reptiles. They have special skin that they shed. They feel dry rather than slimy to the touch.
4. *Unique* means "one of a kind."
5. Answers will vary.

Watery Venice (Card 14)

1. No, they don't.
2. Cars aren't allowed. People get around by walking or by gondolas.
3. Possible answers: Venice is filled with water. It's made up of 118 small islands. There are no cars. People get around in thin boats known as gondolas.
4. *Narrow* means "thin."
5. Possible answer: They need bridges to get across all the canals.

A Very Rare Cat (Card 15)

1. A liger is a mix of a lion and a tiger.
2. The name liger is a combination of two very big cats. Ligers have yellow fur but also stripes.
3. Hercules, the heaviest cat in the world, weighed 922 pounds.
4. *Melding* means "combining."
5. Answers will vary.

Freshwater, Please! (Card 16)

1. No, they can't survive.
2. Seawater is too salty. It doesn't nourish our tissues. It makes people sick.
3. People can't live on seawater because it's too salty.
4. *Vast* means "huge."
5. Possible answer: Bring fresh water, food, and sunscreen.

Steps on the Moon (Card 17)

1. No, people couldn't live on the moon.
2. There is no air or water on the moon.
3. On the moon there's no air or wind or rain or snow.
4. *Ventured* means "traveled."
5. Possible answer: The footprints would not be there because wind or rain would have worn them away.

What Is Wikipedia? (Card 18)

1. Yes, a 10-year-old girl could create a Wikipedia page for her favorite author.
2. Wikipedia is created by the public. Anyone can start a page.
3. Yes, the girl's 8-year-old brother could add new information.
4. *Public* means "people in the community."
5. Answers will vary.

Electric Cars (Card 19)

1. They are better for the environment.
2. Electric cars and hybrids are better for the environment because they use less fuel.
3. Possible answer: Electric cars, which run on electricity, are good for the environment because they use less fuel. They are not a new idea. Thomas Edison worked on one in 1899.
4. *Beneficial* means "helpful."
5. Answers will vary.

A Hare or a Rabbit? (Card 20)

1. A rabbit would make a better pet.
2. Rabbits are gentle and enjoy time with others, but hares are wild.
3. There are many differences between rabbits and hares.
4. *Burrows* means "tunnels."
5. Answers will vary.

Visiting the Vessel (Card 21)

1. The Vessel will likely get a large number of visitors.
2. It's in New York City, and people are excited about it. Other attractions there, such as the Statue of Liberty and the High Line, get large numbers of visitors.
3. The Statue of Liberty is older. The High Line gets more visitors.
4. *Attraction* means "exciting place to visit."
5. Answers will vary.

Animal Symbols (Card 22)

1. Yes, bald eagles live in the U.S.
2. Many countries include animals in their national symbols. They usually choose animals found in that country.
3. Possible answer: Vicuñas are related to llamas and live in Peru.
4. *Majestic* means "amazing."
5. Answers will vary.

It's Hot in Here (Card 23)

1. It's good.
2. A higher temperature helps our bodies fight and beat back the bugs.
3. Fevers aren't bad, because they help our bodies fight off illnesses.
4. *Hospitable* means "friendly."
5. Answers will vary.

Paul, the Celebrity Octopus (Card 24)

1. A German flag was on his food box.
2. The food boxes had team flags. Whatever box Paul ate from counted as his prediction.
3. Germany won seven matches.
4. *Rival* means "competitor."
5. Answers will vary.

Grapes and Raisins (Card 25)

1. You would use a grape to make juice.
2. Grapes are juicy because they have a lot of water. Raisins are dried in the sun, and their water evaporates.
3. Possible answer: They are the same fruit, but grapes are juicy and raisins are dried.
4. *Evaporate* means "turn from liquid to vapor."
5. Answers will vary.

Birds of a Feather (Card 26)

1. An ostrich is a bird.
2. Birds are the only type of creature that has feathers. Some birds can't even fly.
3. What defines a bird is not its wings or whether it can fly or lay eggs. A bird is defined by being the only type of creature that has feathers.
4. *Characteristic* means "specific feature."
5. Answers will vary.

First in Flight (Card 27)

1. Kitty Hawk is in North Carolina.
2. Kitty Hawk is where the Wright brothers made the first flight. North Carolina license plates have the slogan "First in Flight."
3. The Wright brothers' flight lasted 59 seconds, and the plane traveled 852 feet.
4. *Duration* means "amount of time."
5. Answers will vary.

Dual Language (Card 28)

1. *Arrêt* means "stop" in English.
2. In Canada, signs are written in both English and French.
3. In Canada, many signs are in English and French; in the U.S., they're mostly in English.
4. *Region* means "section."
5. Answers will vary.

A Towering Achievement (Card 29)

1. Yes, it's popular with sightseers.
2. Millions of people visit the Eiffel Tower every year.
3. The Eiffel Tower has 108 stories and 1,710 steps.
4. *Ushers* means "guides."
5. Answers will vary.

Bobbie the Wonder Dog (Card 30)

1. Yes, he missed his home and his family.
2. He walked 2,500 miles to get home. His paws were raw.
3. It took Bobbie nine months to return home.
4. *Scrawny* means "skinny."
5. Possible answer: It was a very hard trip. Bobbie didn't have much to eat, because when he got home he was scrawny.

Seeing Inside (Card 31)

1. The X-ray would show marbles.
2. X-rays show what's inside of something. They can show what's inside a bag, a box, or almost anything at all.
3. Possible answer: X-rays were discovered in 1895. X-rays can show what is inside things. Today, they have many different uses, including to look inside bodies, teeth, and containers.
4. *Versatile* means "useful."
5. Answers will vary.

Faster Messages (Card 32)

1. They didn't send texts 50 years ago.
2. The technology wasn't invented yet.
3. Possible answer: People used to send notes in the mail, but now they send texts and emails because they're faster.
4. *Primary* means "main."
5. Answers will vary.

Painter Pablo Picasso (Card 33)

1. Picasso would use light pink.
2. During his Blue Period, he painted everything blue. Then he switched to his Rose Period. Rose means light pink.
3. His Blue Period came first.
4. *Renowned* means "famous."
5. Answers will vary.

Great Big States (Card 34)

1. Rhode Island is a small state.
2. 425 Rhode Islands would fit inside Alaska.
3. The fourth-largest state is Montana. The text says Alaska, Texas, and California are the three biggest, and it says Montana is next after them.
4. *Humongous* means "huge."
5. Answers will vary.

Count the Rings! (Card 35)

1. It was 3,200 years old.
2. Many trees add one growth ring each year.
3. It would be 25 years old.
4. *Towering* means "very tall."
5. Answers will vary.

Unsinkable (Card 36)

1. Yes, she survived.
2. Afterwards, people called her the "Unsinkable Molly Brown."
3. Possible answer: Molly Brown was on the *Titanic* when it sank. She was a hero because she helped people and rowed a lifeboat. Later, she was called the "Unsinkable Molly Brown."
4. *Voyage* means "trip at sea."
5. Answers will vary.

A Funny Frog (Card 37)

1. This frog is called "paradoxical" because it gets smaller as it grows up, and usually it's the opposite.
2. When it's young, it's about 10 inches long, but when it's an adult it's only three and a half inches long.
3. Possible answer: It's nocturnal and it lives in ponds and lakes.
4. *Nocturnal* means "active at night."
5. Answers will vary.

The Metric System (Card 38)
1. It would be a very short distance.
2. A pencil point equals one millimeter. So five millimeters would still be a tiny distance.
3. Inches, feet, and miles are related to the imperial system.
4. *Minuscule* means "tiny."
5. Answers will vary.

Triple Trouble (Card 39)
1. Yes, triple trouble would be more trouble than regular trouble.
2. The word part *tri* means "three." *Triple trouble* means "three times the trouble."
3. Possible answer: *Tri* means "three." Some *tri* words include *triangle*, *trilogy*, *triathlon*, and *triple*.
4. *Distinct* means "separate and different."
5. Answers will vary.

Velkommen to Minnesota! (Card 40)
1. They fished for a job after they moved to Duluth.
2. Many fished for a living in Norway. The text says they could "do the work they love." Duluth, Minnesota, is near Lake Superior, where they could also fish.
3. *Velkommen* means "welcome" in Norwegian.
4. *Immigrate* means "move."
5. Answers will vary.

Meet the Beatles (Card 41)
1. The Beatles had four members.
2. The band was nicknamed the Fab Four. When the Beatles broke up, the Fab Four went their separate ways.
3. The Beatles formed in 1960 and broke up in 1970.
4. *Endured* means "lasted."
5. Answers will vary.

A Long-Ago Long Run (Card 42)
1. A marathon takes its name from an ancient Greek battle.
2. There was an ancient Greek battle called Marathon. Afterwards, a messenger ran a long way to tell of the Greek's victory.
3. He ran about 26 miles.
4. *Victory* means "win."
5. Answers will vary.

Remembering Jackie Robinson (Card 43)
1. They wear number 42.
2. The text says 42 was Jackie Robinson's number. It also says all players wear Jackie Robinson's number on April 15.
3. He retired in 1956.
4. *Figure* means "person."
5. Answers will vary.

Star-Spangled Banner (Card 44)
1. The flag changes when states are added.
2. Arkansas became a state and the number of stars climbed to 25. Hawaii is the 50th state and now the flag has 50 stars.
3. Arkansas became a state first, in 1836. Hawaii became a state in 1959.
4. *Aspects* means "parts or features."
5. Answers will vary.

The Buzz About Bees (Card 45)
1. They probably don't get stung very much.
2. They wear special clothes and gloves and a net over their faces.
3. Bees help produce honey, apples, pears, peaches, almonds, and cantaloupes.
4. *Protective* means "safe."
5. Answers will vary.

Krakatoa! (Card 46)

1. The Krakatoa volcano caused the red sunset in New Haven, CT.
2. Krakatoa caused red sunsets in places as far away as America.
3. Possible answer: Krakatoa erupted in 1883. The big eruption caused sunsets all over the world to be unusually red.
4. *Vivid* means "powerful."
5. Possible answer: No, I don't think anyone made a video of Krakatoa erupting because video cameras were not invented yet.

False Names (Card 47)

1. Theodor Seuss Geisel's pseudonym is Dr. Seuss.
2. A pseudonym is a made-up name for a writer. Theodor Seuss Geisel's books all said "by Dr. Seuss."
3. Daniel Handler is the real name of the author of the Lemony Snicket books.
4. *Classic* means "outstanding and remembered."
5. Answers will vary.

Cartoon Creation (Card 48)

1. Yes, it does require teamwork.
2. It takes a lot of people, and there are a lot of steps.
3. Possible answer: The writers write a good story. Then, the actors perform the lines. Next, images are drawn. Lastly, all the pieces are put together.
4. *Images* means "pictures."
5. Answers will vary.

Eat Your Spinach! (Card 49)

1. An orange is more nutritious.
2. Fruits are packed with vitamins. Chips aren't very nutritious.
3. Fruits and vegetables are really good for you.
4. *Nutritious* means "healthy."
5. Answers will vary.

Gold! (Card 50)

1. No, the Gold Rush did not make lots of people rich.
2. Most people moved to California and their dreams didn't come true.
3. More than 300,000 people went to California to dig for gold.
4. *Majority* means "larger number."
5. Possible answer: James Marshall wanted to keep his discovery a secret so that people would not come and look for gold. He wanted to keep all the gold for himself.

INFERENCE: LITERARY

That's Spicy! (Card 51)

1. No, he didn't enjoy them.
2. They were too spicy. His mouth was on fire, and he wanted to have some of his sister's mild tacos instead.
3. Possible answer: No, he will probably order medium or mild.
4. *Ablaze* means "on fire."
5. Possible answer: His mom thinks that the tacos will be too spicy for Eric.

Harry's Haircut (Card 52)

1. He's unhappy with his haircut.
2. He looked in the mirror and his heart sank. He bites his lip when speaking to the barber. He nervously asks his mom what she thinks.
3. Harry's mom didn't like the haircut either, because she said, "Well, the good news is that your hair grows very quickly."
4. *Unruly* means "messy."
5. Answers will vary.

Sania's Snowman (Card 53)

1. She used candies for the eyes.
2. Sid was eating shiny blue candy. The snowman's eyes were shiny blue.
3. The story is set in Montana. It is winter.
4. *Suitable* means "correct."
5. Answers will vary.

The Blueberry Fan (Card 54)

1. Yes, she does.
2. She picked a bunch of blueberries to make her sister happy.
3. Possible answers: The tone is funny, playful, lighthearted, teasing.
4. *Elated* means "happy."
5. Answers will vary.

Last-Leaf Lenny (Card 55)

1. He landed in the pile of leaves.
2. He wanted to join his friends in the leaf pile. He changed color, snapped off the tree, and floated down.
3. The theme of the story is "good things come to those who wait." Lenny waited, but then he got to join his friends.
4. *Hue* means "color."
5. Answers will vary.

The Sandwich Sneak (Card 56)

1. Stu ate Lucy's sandwich.
2. It was Stu because his top lip was brown and purple from peanut butter and jelly.
3. It takes place in a kitchen.
4. *Livid* means "very mad."
5. Answers will vary.

An Ice Cream Day (Card 57)

1. The ice cream melted.
2. Noah thought, "Uh-oh," and then his heart sank when his mom asked if he'd put it back in the freezer.
3. The ice cream was Super-Fudgy-Ripple.
4. *Declared* means "said."
5. Answers will vary.

Ping-Pong Problem (Card 58)

1. Jason lost the game.
2. Jason dropped his paddle and threw up his arms. Then he stormed out of the basement frowning.
3. Jason is a poor sport. He got upset when he lost. Then he told Jill he could beat her at the video game.
4. *Lunged* means "moved suddenly forward."
5. Answers will vary.

First Time Sledding (Card 59)

1. Gina is excited.
2. Gina has a fluttery feeling in her stomach. She can't sleep. She jumps out of bed the next day. She wants her cousin to wake up.
3. It doesn't snow in Florida. I know because Gina lived there and has never seen snow.
4. *Peered* means "looked."
5. Answers will vary.

Wanda Is Wild for Wolves (Card 60)

1. The wrapping paper is covered with wolves.
2. Wanda loves wolves. Among other things, she has wolf cups and wolf pajamas, and she watches wolf movies.
3. The tone is humorous.
4. *Depiction* means "picture."
5. Answers will vary.

Candy Overload (Card 61)

1. Oliver ate too much candy and got sick.
2. When Oliver thought back to last Halloween his stomach began to hurt.
3. Possible answer: His mom is wise, kind, and thoughtful.
4. *Brimming* means "filled."
5. Answers will vary.

Smooth Sailing? (Card 62)

1. Deena was not having a good time.
2. She felt queasy and asked her grandfather when they could go home.
3. She probably won't go sailing again because she didn't have a good time.
4. *Queasy* means "nauseated."
5. Answers will vary.

Third Time's the Charm (Card 63)

1. Juan makes a swan.
2. The text says that Juan's creation looks perfect. Also, Juan says, "The third time's the charm."
3. Juan says "The third times the charm" because it takes him three tries to make a swan.
4. *Resemble* means "look like."
5. Answers will vary.

Bad Planning (Card 64)

1. Yes, she does.
2. Iris hates getting wet and it starts to rain. She screams and can't fit under Jake's umbrella.
3. It's good to be prepared.
4. *Cautioned* means "warned."
5. Answers will vary.

Marble Magic (Card 65)

1. Gina was thinking of 7.
2. She was astonished and let out a surprised laugh when Joel showed her seven marbles. Then Joel said, "Wow, I guess I REALLY am magic!"
3. Possible answer: Joel is young, goofy, and enthusiastic.
4. *Astonished* means "amazed."
5. Answers will vary.

The Birthday Dinner (Card 66)

1. Bart is getting cabbage.
2. Bart's mom is burning a scented candle to hide the smell of cabbage.
3. Bart's mother is thoughtful. You can tell because she burns a rose-smelling candle and makes Bart's favorite food, cabbage, for his birthday.
4. *Mask* means "hide."
5. Answers will vary.

Bad Table Manners (Card 67)

1. In this story, a spoon could talk.
2. A knife, a glass, a salt shaker, and other items on the table can talk, so I think a spoon would be able to talk, too.
3. Possible answer: The tone of this story is silly and zany.
4. *Retorted* means "sharply answered."
5. Answers will vary.

B-Ball Turnaround (Card 68)

1. She feels happy.
2. She leaps into the air and doesn't stop smiling for days.
3. Possible answer: She's patient, hard-working, and dedicated.
4. *Seldom* means "rarely."
5. Answers will vary.

Sweet Relief (Card 69)

1. Nia doesn't like it.
2. Nia stays underwater as long as she can just to avoid hearing Jordan sing the song again.
3. Possible answer: Jordan will be bouncing up and down on the diving board singing the song.
4. *Incessantly* means "constantly."
5. Answers will vary.

The Pipers Pick Their Pumpkins (Card 70)

1. Perry Piper got the smallest pumpkin.
2. The bigger the family member, the larger the pumpkin. Perry must be the smallest because he's still a toddler.
3. It takes place in the fall. I know because it is Halloween.
4. *Grimace* means "scowl."
5. Answers will vary.

Lost and Found (Card 71)

1. No, Milo is not.
2. He lost so many things, such as a calculator, a sweater, a hat, headphones, and his wallet.
3. Possible answer: I predict he will lose them again.
4. *Departed* means "left."
5. Answers will vary.

The Favorite (Card 72)

1. It's a cat.
2. Because it chases the silly dog, curls up in a ball, and purrs.
3. Possible answer: The tone is funny or playful.
4. *Vault* means "jump."
5. Answers will vary.

Freckle Face (Card 73)

1. At the start of the story, Katy doesn't like freckles.
2. Katy says she wishes she could wash away her freckles. She also mentions that kids were teasing her.
3. At the end of the story, Katy does like freckles. She says to her mom, "You've made me change my mind about freckles . . . again."
4. *Inquired* means "asked."
5. Answers will vary.

A Snowy Walk (Card 74)

1. They took the path on the left.
2. Penny's paw prints are in the snow on the path to the left, and Sean says, "Let's take the path Penny took."
3. It's winter, because there is snow.
4. *Sprinted* means "ran."
5. Sean lives in the country. I know because the text mentions woods and a barn.

Rapunzel's New Hairdo (Card 75)

1. Now Rapunzel's hair is too short.
2. The text says, "Snip, snip." The Prince couldn't reach her hair. It hung only a little way down the tower wall.
3. The Prince is not deeply in love with Rapunzel, because they hang out reading and playing video games.
4. *Exceedingly* means "very."
5. Answers will vary.

Untitled Tale (Card 76)

1. Thelma Thumb is tiny.
2. Her name is Thelma Thumb, and she sails on a leaf, climbs up an anthill, and hikes through tall grass blades. A few potato chip crumbs are enough food for a week.
3. Possible answer: Thelma would live in a tiny house. It might be made of toothpicks with a roof made out of a candy wrapper.
4. *Epic* means "big and heroic."
5. Answers will vary.

Postponed (Card 77)

1. He says they will go next weekend because Jamal is sick.
2. Jamal is sneezing and coughing and he might have a fever.
3. It takes place in the morning.
4. *Thunderous* means "very loud."
5. Possible answer: It's called "Postponed" because they will have to go to the amusement park another day.

The Right Horse (Card 78)

1. Brie is a talented and experienced horseback rider.
2. Brie chose Pepper, the ornery horse. But Brie was firm with the reins and talked to Pepper in a confident voice. Soon, Pepper began to behave.
3. Possible answer: Pepper would keep running and maybe the rider would fall off.
4. *Ornery* means "bad-tempered."
5. Answers will vary.

The Legend of Rooster (Card 79)

1. It is sunrise.
2. Cow told Rooster not to talk until sunrise. The text says, "It was finally time to tell Cow."
3. The setting is a farm.
4. *Jumbled* means "mixed up."
5. Answers will vary.

Weird World of Sports (Card 80)

1. Baxter Beaver uses his tail.
2. Baxter Beaver's tail is wide and powerful. When he swings it, the other tennis players don't stand a chance.
3. I think Sandy Shark will win because the text says she is undefeated.
4. *Formidable* means "impressive."
5. Answers will vary.

Good Things Come in Small and Large Packages (Card 81)

1. Mia's mother got a ring.
2. These are the clues: The gift came in a tiny box. She put it on her finger. It sparkled.
3. I think the gift cost $20, because Mia used a month's allowance, which likely wouldn't be $20,000!
4. *Mammoth* means "very large."
5. Answers will vary.

The Baby Birds (Card 82)

1. They flew away.
2. The birds were getting bigger and practicing flapping their wings.
3. Possible answer: Aki is curious, kind, and interested in nature.
4. *Fledglings* means "baby birds."
5. Answers will vary.

The Present (Card 83)

1. Micah is waiting for the mail carrier.
2. He keeps looking up and down the block for the mail carrier.
3. I think it's a scooter for Micah because the truck says "Dave's Scooter Shop."
4. *Glanced* means "looked."
5. Answers will vary.

Opposite Man (Card 84)

1. No, he is not brave.
2. Superheroes are brave. Opposite Man is the opposite of a typical superhero.
3. Yes, Opposite Man would help a bank robber because he helps villains.
4. *Villains* means "bad guys."
5. Answers will vary.

A Baking Flop (Card 85)

1. Yeast makes bread rise and not be flat.
2. Jewel left out the yeast and her bread was flat.
3. It takes place in the kitchen of a home.
4. *Basic* means "simple."
5. Answers will vary.

Messy Mo (Card 86)

1. She knows her mom is going to be mad.
2. Her mom told her to make sure Mo didn't get dirty, and he left paw prints on the sofa.
3. Possible answer: I think Mo has to go outside and Yasmin has to clean up the mess.
4. *Scampered* means "ran."
5. Answers will vary.

Blooming Daffodils (Card 87)

1. Lorenzo sees daffodils.
2. Several months have passed, and it's time for the flowers to bloom. Also, he sees a bright yellow patch.
3. The season is spring. Daffodils bloom in spring.
4. *Detected* means "noticed."
5. Answers will vary.

I Don't Want to Go to Sleep! (Card 88)

1. Her mother knows better.
2. Ruby falls asleep. Her mother knows there's no food and they have to save their energy.
3. Possible answer: She's adventurous and wants to have fun.
4. *Hibernate* means "sleep during winter."
5. Answers will vary.

A Perfect Birthday (Card 89)

1. They're at the movies.
2. They buy popcorn. Then the lights dim and the screen comes to life.
3. They watch the movie.
4. *Dimmed* means "got darker."
5. Answers will vary.

Sleepyhead (Card 90)

1. She stayed up too late the night before.
2. She kept reading, even though it was past her bedtime.
3. It gets her up because it's really loud.
4. *Slumbering* means "sleeping."
5. Answers will vary.

The Recital (Card 91)
1. No, it does not go as he planned.
2. Felipe made lots of mistakes. He wished he had listened to Jackie and practiced more.
3. I predict that Felipe will practice a lot before his next recital.
4. *Challenging* means "hard."
5. Possible answer: I learned that practice makes perfect.

How Will I Do It? (Card 92)
1. Yes, Clarence becomes a butterfly.
2. Clarence goes through all the stages, and in the end he has beautiful wings.
3. Clarence is nervous and worried.
4. *Anxiously* means "nervously."
5. Answers will vary.

Raccoon Tan (Card 93)
1. Mila wore her new goggles.
2. Mila was at the beach all day. The goggles must have blocked the sun, creating white circles around her eyes.
3. It takes place at an ocean beach.
4. *Transformed* means "totally changed."
5. Answers will vary.

A Bad School Day (Card 94)
1. No, Jasmine had a bad day when she returned to school.
2. Kristi didn't pick Jasmine to be her math partner, and she ate her lunch with Elena. At the end of the story, Jasmine just frowns.
3. Possible answer: Jasmine feels sad, left out, and lonely.
4. *Inseparable* means "always together."
5. Answers will vary.

Is It Broken? (Card 95)
1. No, Anika's arm is not broken.
2. The doctor says "Good news" and tells her she just has to rest it for a few days.
3. The story ends in a hospital emergency room.
4. *Gingerly* means "carefully."
5. Answers will vary.

Time-Traveling Tomás (Card 96)
1. Tomás decided to stay in the present.
2. There were cars, buildings, and people on cellphones.
3. Yes. Dinosaurs were everywhere, and they're from way back in time.
4. *Menacing* means "threatening."
5. Answers will vary.

Wendy's Walls (Card 97)
1. Wendy can't decide on a color.
2. She changes her mind many times. She sighs at the end of the story.
3. Possible answers: She can't make up her mind.
4. *Indecisive* means "unable to decide."
5. Answers will vary.

Eye Trouble (Card 98)
1. Hector goes into a glasses store.
2. He's having trouble seeing clearly. It's hard for him to read the whiteboard in class, and movies look blurry.
3. The story takes place at a mall.
4. *Squint* means "close eyes partway."
5. Answers will vary.

Jaycee at the Bat (Card 99)

1. Jaycee hit a home run.
2. Jaycee hit the ball hard. Afterwards, she just kept running until she reached home plate. Her teammates were jumping up and down. Her coach was proud. Even her little brother cheered.
3. I predict that the other team was sad, because they lost the game.
4. *Hearty* means "strong and loud."
5. Answers will vary.

A Trip to the Doctor (Card 100)

1. Adam is scared.
2. When his mom tells him he has to get one, his heart beats fast and his knees shake. He also stammers.
3. Possible answer: Adam tries to act brave, but he is a scaredy-cat, too.
4. *Tremble* means "shake."
5. Answers will vary.